The Masculine Edge:

A Field Guide to Strength and Character

Dr Chuck Carrington

This is a nonfiction work. However, certain sections have been lightly fictionalized or dramatized for illustrative purposes. Any resemblance to actual persons, living or deceased, is purely coincidental.

Copyright © 2025 CP Carrington
all rights reserved
ISBN 979-8-9892386-4-4 (paperback edition)
Printed by Connect Books in the United States of America

Connect Books
USA

PO BOX 903 Wakefield VA. USA 23888
Connectbooks.pub

Scripture quotations are from the King James Version of the Bible. Public domain.

All rights reserved. No part of this book may be reproduced in any form or by an electronic or mechanical means, including information storage and retrieval systems, without permission in writing from the publisher, except by a reviewer who may quote brief passages in a review.

Dedication

To the *inner circle:* Mike, Hans, Drew, David, Ryan and Charles, and all the members from Overcomers, Men of Valor, and Covenant Men who I have come to know and love over the past 15 years. These stories have circulated through our sustained conversation for a long time. It is overdue that we now offer them to outsiders. Thanks for teaching me as much as I have taught you.

Acknowledgements

To Larry Mast—without his sharp eye and steady editorial guidance, I'd still be lost in a dyslexic fugue of doubt. I am deeply grateful.

-and-

To the men who volunteered to be the readers of the raw book, thank you for slogging through my ramblings!

Contents

Building a Sharp Edge 1

The Conversation of Your Life 5

Putting the Horse Before the Cart 15

What Lies Beneath: The Goals of Misbehavior 25

Carrying the Banner 53

Attend to the Tree Not the Fruit 67

Fruit From a Poisoned Tree 77

Feeding The Hungry Man 89

Tomorrow For Sure! 95

Maybe it's time to Pop the Hood 105

The Truth Shall Set You Free 117

Thinking Outside What Box? 129

Trigger Points..137

Less is More & When to Not To… 147

Endless Exhaustion:..169

Would You Let Your Son Do That? 177

Are You A David, or an Albert? 187

You Don't Say..195

Change Happens In An Instant...207

Great Marriages Don't Just Happen 211

Raising the Banner Daily 215

Carry the Flame 219

4

Building a Sharp Edge
Using this Book

I have compiled this book specifically for men. It is a collection of just some of the many conversations men and I have had over the last ten or so years in our various counseling groups. I have distilled them into topics and tried to make them interesting and relevant so I don't lose your attention, because, as a fellow male on the journey of life, I know how A.D.D. we all can be. Which is also why I am reluctant to record this as an audiobook, despite the massive number of requests I have received to do so.

To get the most out of **The Masculine Edge**, please do not sit down and read it through like a novel. This will not be a marathon read, or a cramming of information just to get a task accomplished. Not if you want to actually get somewhere. Treat it like you are sitting in one of our counseling groups, discipleship groups, or men's retreats where we tend to talk about these topics. Read a "chapter" and then ponder the questions I have put at the end in the *Field Notes* section. It really is that simple. You can use this book like a weekly devotional. Read a chapter, ponder it, practice it for the following week, then read the next chapter. Over time, you will produce an outcome.

Below is an example of a completed *Field Note* just to show you how simple I intend this to be.

(Example from the Chapter: You Don't Say)

Field Notes: You Don't Say

1. Situation Report:

Where did this chapter hit home for me?

> I thought about the way I've been emotionally distant with my son, especially lately. I assume he knows I love him, but I haven't said it.

2. Operational Insight:

What truth or principle stands out to me the most?

State it in your own words. Keep it simple.

> Silence isn't neutral. It can hurt just as much as harsh words.

3. Action Step:

What's one small thing I will do differently this week because of this chapter?

Think action, not theory.

> I'll tell my son this weekend, out loud, "I'm proud of you and I love you."

4. Words to Say:

Who needs to hear something from me?

> To my wife: "You're the best part of my life, and I'm grateful for you."

5. Brief Prayer:

Write a one-sentence prayer asking God to strengthen your character in this area.

> Lord, teach me to use my words like You do—to bring life and not just fill silence.

Remember, I am a guy too. So I get it. No one wants another task added to his already busy life. Keep it simple, but mean what you write, and then act it out all week.

.

The Conversation of Your Life

A man's life is never silent—his actions, habits, and daily choices are always communicating what he truly values. According to Scripture, "conversation" refers not merely to speech but to one's manner of life. Every man, therefore, is a living message, declaring either integrity or compromise, sacred devotion or self-centered rebellion. This chapter calls men to recognize the broadcast of their lives and bring it into alignment with the gospel of Christ.

"Only let your conversation be as it becometh the gospel of Christ…"
— Philippians 1:27 (KJV)

You Cannot *Not* Communicate

Whether you realize it or not, you are always saying something. Even when you're silent, you're broadcasting. Your face, your posture, your spending, your work ethic, your habits—they all communicate. A father who never says, "I love you" to his kids still communicates volumes by what he prioritizes. A husband who rarely speaks to his wife still sends a message with every choice he makes about time, attention, and effort. A man who calls himself a follower of Christ but never opens his Bible, prays, or lives with moral integrity is making a statement too—a loud one.

In the field of communication, there's a foundational principle: *"You cannot not communicate."* Silence is communication. Absence is communication. So is a sigh, a frown, a broken promise, and a raised voice. Men are broadcasting their beliefs all the time, whether they intend to or not. And this is exactly what the Bible means when it speaks of your "conversation."

Conversation Is More Than Words

In several places, the King James Bible uses the word *conversation* in a way that surprises modern readers. We usually think of conversation as a verbal exchange. But in Scripture, the word often refers to your *manner of life*, your *conduct*, your *lifestyle*. It is how you live, not just how you speak.

- **Philippians 1:27** – *"Only let your conversation be as it becometh the gospel of Christ."*
    - The Greek word here, *politeuomai*, means to behave as a citizen. Paul is saying, "Live in such a way that your life aligns with your heavenly citizenship."

- **Hebrews 13:5** – *"Let your conversation be without covetousness…"*
    - The writer uses *tropos*, referring to a habitual way of life. The message? Live in a way that reflects contentment and trust in God.

- **1 Peter 1:15** – *"Be ye holy in all manner of conversation."*
    - The Greek *anastrophē* means lifestyle, conduct, way of behaving.

- **1 Peter 3:1-2** – Wives are told to win over their husbands "by the conversation" of their lives—not their arguments, but their character.

These passages make something profoundly clear: your life *is* your message.

Your Life Is Always Speaking

Whether you're aware of it or not, your conduct declares what you believe, what you value, and who you really are. You can wear a cross around your neck, but your attitude toward your wife and your kids reveals your theology far more accurately. You can post Scripture on social media, but if your coworkers know you as lazy, crude, or dishonest, you've preached a far louder message than you realize.

Your life is a pulpit.

Every man you meet is reading your manner of life like a sermon. Your children are watching how you treat their mother. Your wife sees whether you practice what you preach. Your friends know whether you're consistent when no one's watching. The cashier notices whether you speak kindly when your order is wrong. Your time, your money, your words, your eyes—they are all saying something. And what they say reveals what is sacred to you.

What You Hold Sacred Will Show

Jesus said, *"Where your treasure is, there will your heart be also"* (Matt. 6:21). That's not just about money—it's about attention, focus, energy, and value. Whatever you hold sacred will shape your life. And because of that, it will show up in your conversation—your way of living.

A man who holds comfort sacred will avoid hardship. A man who holds status sacred will chase appearance. A man who holds God sacred will order his life in reverence.

In Proverbs 4:23, we're told to guard our heart because *"out of it are the issues of life."* Everything you do flows from your internal values. And those values are constantly visible in how you live. You don't have to tell anyone what you love. They can already see it.

When Words and Witness Don't Match

Too many Christian men suffer from spiritual dissonance—their lips speak one message while their life shouts another. We have grown comfortable with saying the right things while excusing the fact that we're living the wrong way.

We lead men's Bible studies and then explode in anger at home. We pray in church and then ignore our wives for days. We give money to missions but won't apologize to our kids. This hypocrisy is not lost on those around us. It wounds trust. It confuses others. And it tarnishes the name of Christ.

Paul warned in Romans 2:24 that *"the name of God is blasphemed among the Gentiles through you."*

Character isn't declared—it's demonstrated. And your life is either confirming your message or canceling it.

A Gospel-Shaped Life

Philippians 1:27 calls us to let our *conversation be as it becometh the gospel of Christ.* That means we are to live in a way that *adorns* the message we claim to believe. We are not just gospel *believers*—we are gospel *representatives*. Your life should show grace, truth, integrity, humility, strength, and love.

Ask yourself:

- Does my life show that Christ is King?
- Does my marriage reflect the gospel?
- Does my daily conduct point others to Jesus?

You are either a living billboard for Christ, or a walking disclaimer that warns, "Do not take this man seriously."

The Power of Silent Witness

Some of the strongest sermons are preached in silence.

In 1 Peter 3, wives are told they may win their husbands without a word—*"by the conversation of their lives."* That same principle applies to men. Some of the most compelling witnesses are not loud or charismatic. They are steady. Dependable. Godly. Faithful.

When a man refuses to cheat at work, speaks gently to his wife, disciplines his kids in love, and remains humble and kind under pressure—he preaches a message that no sermon can improve.

The world is not looking for perfect men. They are looking for *authentic* ones.

Aligning Your Life with Your Message

So how do you bring your conversation in line with your convictions?

1. **Examine Your Habits** – Your routines speak louder than your goals.
2. **Evaluate Your Speech** – Not just words, but the tone, timing, and spirit behind them.
3. **Audit Your Time** – Your calendar reveals your true priorities.
4. **Strengthen Your Disciplines** – What you do in private will shape who you are in public.

5. **Submit to Discipleship** – You need men who will tell you the truth.

Consistency is king. The goal is not perfection but integrity—living a life where what you say and what you do are pointing in the same direction.

If You Need a Reset

Maybe your life has been telling the wrong story. Maybe your "conversation" has not reflected Christ. The good news is that repentance is still an option. God's mercy is not just for our failures but for our transformation.

It's not too late to change your message. Confess where your conduct has fallen short. Seek forgiveness from those you've misled or hurt. Realign your habits to reflect what is truly sacred.

What Is Your Life Saying? Your life is talking, brother. It's either saying, *"Christ is Lord"* or *"I am."* It's either declaring integrity or displaying compromise. It's either upholding what is sacred or trampling it for convenience. Let your *conversation*—your conduct, your character, your choices—be as it becomes the gospel of Christ. Because the world is listening. And more importantly, so is God.

Field Notes:

1. Situation Report:
Where did this chapter hit home for me?

2. Operational Insight:
What truth or principle stands out to me the most?

3. Action Step:
What's one small thing I will do differently this week because of this chapter?

4. Words to Say:
Who needs to hear something from me?

5. Brief Prayer:
Write a one-sentence prayer asking God to strengthen your character in this area.

Putting the Horse Before the Cart

Restoring Order and Unity in the Unequally Yoked Marriage

"Can two walk together, unless they are agreed?" (Amos 3:3)

It's a piercing question, and one that reaches past casual acquaintance into the core of any meaningful relationship, especially marriage. Agreement is not about thinking identically—it's about intentional alignment. Two people can have different backgrounds, perspectives, or preferences, but if they are not committed to walking in agreement, they are not truly walking together. They're simply sharing a road while moving in opposite directions.

Consider for a moment a couple—let's call them Josh and Emily. From the outside, they look like they've got everything together. Two kids, a mortgage, stable jobs, Sunday church attendance. But inside the walls of their home, there's a slow erosion happening. They never actually *agree* on anything substantial. They've learned to avoid topics instead of resolving them. When finances come up, she takes control because she doesn't trust him to be responsible. When parenting issues arise, he shrinks back, because every opinion he offers gets overruled. They're not yelling, not throwing plates. But they're not walking together either. And over time, that distance accumulates into something more than silence—it becomes disunity. And where there is disunity, there is no peace.

This disunity is a symptom of something deeper, something more foundational: the order of their relationship has been reversed. The cart has been put before the horse. And no matter how sincere their intentions or how noble their efforts, they are working against a design that God Himself established.

The old proverb says, "Don't get the cart before the horse." It's simple wisdom, yet profound when you stop to think about how often we do just that in our relationships. You wouldn't expect a wagon to move forward with the load in front and the engine behind. It would be foolishness to even try. But modern marriages are full of this kind of foolishness—not because people are foolish, but because culture has convinced us to ignore the design.

Take, for example, a couple in the early stages of marriage. They want to do things "equally." So, when a decision needs to be made—whether to relocate, how to discipline a child, how to handle in-laws—they believe every choice must be 50/50. If agreement isn't reached, they either stall indefinitely or resort to the default cultural scripts: "Well, this must mean we're incompatible" or "Maybe we weren't meant to be married." The very presence of disagreement becomes evidence, in their minds, that the marriage is defective.

But Scripture offers a different paradigm: **if you are married, find agreement**. If you are bound in covenant, your task is not to preserve individual preferences at all costs, but to pursue unity—even if that means yielding, repenting, adjusting, or leading when it's difficult.

Let's talk plainly: a lot of marriages today are "unequally yoked," not just between believer and unbeliever, but between two people who never established or maintained biblical roles. Many Christian men, in particular, have abdicated leadership—not because they're lazy, but because they fear conflict. They've bought the lie that leadership equals domination, and in an effort to avoid being labeled controlling or misogynistic, they've laid down their authority entirely. So, decisions go unmade, direction becomes unclear, and their wives step into the void—not because they want to dominate, but because someone has to steer the ship.

Let's paint a scene. A wife is tired. She's making 90% of the decisions, from the kids' schooling to how much they tithe. Her husband says he's "fine with whatever," but when things go wrong, he gets bitter or resentful. She feels alone. She doesn't want to lead, but he won't. She begins to lose respect, not just for his decisions, but for his silence. Over time, she starts making decisions without him—not out of rebellion, but out of survival.

Here's the danger: when a man abdicates leadership, a vacuum forms. And in most cases, it gets filled by someone who wasn't meant to carry it alone. The burden exhausts both parties. The man feels irrelevant. The woman feels unsupported. And neither feels known.

This isn't a hypothetical. This is happening every day, in the pews of Bible-believing churches, in homes where Scripture is quoted but not applied. And it doesn't stop with abdication.

Another issue is the distortion of leadership roles by cultural feminism. This is where the narrative flips entirely. Not only should men not lead—women *must* lead. Because women are said to be more emotionally intelligent, more nurturing, and simply more competent. Leadership is no longer a shared spiritual responsibility—it's a turf war.

In these homes, the husband is often belittled. His input is seen as quaint. He's expected to provide financially, but not to guide spiritually or administratively. If he asserts himself, he's told he's being oppressive. If he retreats, he's accused of being passive. It's a no-win situation unless he's willing to reassert godly leadership—not by overpowering, but by out serving.

But here's the twist—sometimes the wife doesn't even *want* that level of control. The cultural script told her she should, but she finds it lonely. She finds it exhausting. Deep down, many women long for their husbands to lead—but to do it with humility, courage, and consistency.

Then we hit the third layer: the modern idea of "equality" in marriage means there can be no clear leader. Because leadership implies hierarchy, and hierarchy has become a dirty word. And if there *must* be a leader, many argue it should be the woman, because "she's the one who's actually doing all the work in the home anyway."

But biblical marriage is not a democracy where both parties have equal veto power until consensus is reached. Nor is it a dictatorship where one voice dominates the other. It's a covenant. It's a spiritual structure with Christ as the head, the husband as the servant-leader, and the wife as the trusted helpmate and co-laborer. Not a doormat. Not a puppet. A partner, submitted to God and secure in her husband's love.

When this gets inverted, everything else suffers. Discipline of children becomes inconsistent. Finances get mishandled. Decisions about church involvement, job opportunities, and even conflict resolution become battlegrounds of unspoken resentment rather than places of unity.

Worse still is how disagreements are handled. In modern culture, the existence of conflict is viewed as a failure of compatibility. The line "If we can't agree, maybe we shouldn't be married" gets thrown around like a grenade—destructive, reactive, and often manipulative. Divorce, separation, and emotional detachment become tools for power rather than last resorts.

I've known couples where the phrase "I'll just leave" gets tossed out during every heated argument. It's not said with seriousness, but with threat. It's not about ending the marriage—it's about winning the moment. And when this becomes a habit, it trains both people to see disagreement as dangerous, rather than as an opportunity to grow in grace.

Contrast that with God's view: "You are married. So find agreement." Full stop.

That means staying at the table. That means wrestling through issues, even the messy ones. That means not just asking, "What do I want?" but "What would honor God?" and "What would serve my spouse?"

It also means knowing when to yield—not out of defeat, but out of trust. Biblical submission is not about inferiority. It's about functional order. The wife, in choosing to submit, does so not because her husband is always right, but because she trusts God's design. The husband, in choosing to lead, does so not because he wants control, but because he knows he is accountable before God.

Now let's return to the horse and cart analogy. The **marriage** is the **horse**. It is the source of strength, the means of movement. It is the commitment that pulls the load of life. The **agreement** is the **cart**—the outcome, the fruit, the evidence of unity. When you make agreement the horse, you turn the covenant into a contract. You say, "I will stay with you *if* we continue to agree." That's not covenant—that's convenience. And when the inevitable seasons of misunderstanding, frustration, or fatigue hit—and they *will*—you'll be tempted to unhook the cart and look for another road. But when marriage is the horse—when covenant leads—you stay connected even when the load gets heavy. You pull together even when the road is uphill. You say, "We *will* find a way forward, because this bond matters more than our momentary preferences."

What does that look like practically? It looks like a husband inviting his wife's opinion, considering it carefully, and then making a decision in prayer and humility—even if it's not popular. It looks like a wife expressing her concerns honestly, but also saying, "I trust you," even when the outcome is uncertain. It looks like both parties repenting quickly. Saying sorry first. Asking God together, "What do You want in this situation?" It looks like praying when you don't want to. It looks like going to counseling when you'd rather not. It looks like choosing unity over ego, and covenant over comfort.

If you've been living in a marriage where the cart is leading the horse, there's good news: it's not too late to turn around. The road to restoration starts with one person deciding to realign with God's design. One person choosing to lead, not with volume but with virtue. One person choosing to submit, not with resentment but with reverence. And in time, what feels like drudgery can become delight. What was disunity can become deep agreement. Not because every difference is erased, but because both hearts are yoked to the same purpose: to glorify God in their marriage, and to walk together in unity.

Let us remember: the horse must pull the cart. The covenant must pull the effort toward agreement. Get the order right, and the journey becomes possible. Keep it reversed, and all you'll feel is resistance. So lead. Submit. Forgive. Seek agreement. And let your marriage move forward—not by the strength of your personality, but by the order of God's design.

Field Notes:

1. Situation Report:
Where did this chapter hit home for me?

2. Operational Insight:
What truth or principle stands out to me the most?

3. Action Step:
What's one small thing I will do differently this week because of this chapter?

4. Words to Say:
Who needs to hear something from me?

5. Brief Prayer:
Write a one-sentence prayer asking God to strengthen your character in this area.

What Lies Beneath: The Goals of Misbehavior

When we think of misbehavior, our minds often jump to children—tantrums, defiance, eye-rolling teenagers slamming doors. Rarely do we extend the term to adults, especially not to ourselves. But misbehavior doesn't age out. It simply evolves. It gets dressed up in more socially acceptable forms: sarcasm, withdrawal, passive-aggression, cold shoulders, control, self-pity. Adults misbehave too—especially in relationships. And often, we're just as unaware of the root causes as the child stomping their feet in the cereal aisle.

Alfred Adler, one of the most influential figures in modern psychology, proposed that all behavior—even misbehavior—is goal-directed. People act out not because they are irrational or evil but because they are trying to meet a need. Dinkmeyer and McKay[1], in their work *Systematic Training for Effective Parenting of Teens* (STEP-Teens), expanded on Adler's foundational ideas, laying out four distinct goals of misbehavior: **attention**, **power**, **revenge**, and **inadequacy**. When applied to parenting, these goals help adults understand why their children behave the way they do. But the wisdom doesn't stop at adolescence.

In this chapter, we'll explore how these same four goals explain much of the misbehavior between *adults* in intimate relationships—especially marriage—and how understanding them can transform how we respond to conflict, hurt, and disconnection.

Let's start where most conflict begins: feeling unseen.

1. The Goal of Attention: "See Me"

In a quiet house, a wife sighs loudly for the third time in a row. Her husband, seated nearby, continues scrolling on his phone. She makes a passive comment about the dishes. No response. She asks if he's heard her. He looks up briefly and says, "What?"

He's not trying to hurt her. He's just tired. But that sigh wasn't about the dishes. It was a signal flare. "Notice me. Hear me. Feel what I feel." When she doesn't get the attention she craves, her behavior escalates. She starts to

---

[1] Systematic Training for Effective Parenting of Teens (STEP-Teens),

criticize, to nitpick. Maybe she even becomes clingy or emotional at times that feel disproportionate.

This is the first goal of misbehavior: **attention**.

Adults who seek attention aren't shallow—they're starving. Somewhere along the way, they learned that the only way to be valued is to be noticed. If positive attention isn't available, negative attention will do. This is why some spouses pick fights they don't actually care about—because a shouting match is at least a connection.

A man, for example, might begin working longer hours, not because the job demands it, but because he wants his wife to notice how hard he works. When she doesn't say anything, he might start complaining about how underappreciated he feels or begin comparing himself to "so-and-so's husband." The underlying message isn't really about the job—it's "I want to matter."

What makes attention-seeking behavior so dangerous in relationships is that it often elicits **annoyance** or **withdrawal** from the partner. And that response reinforces the original feeling of neglect. The cycle deepens.

The Healthy Response: The antidote isn't to flood your spouse with shallow compliments or give in to every plea for reassurance. It's to develop rhythms of *intentional* presence. Listen fully when they speak. Notice small details. Express appreciation *consistently*. And when misbehavior crops up, try to ask yourself, "Is this behavior a cry for connection?" Then, instead of *reacting* to the behavior, *respond* to the need underneath it.

2. The Goal of Power: "You Will Not Control Me"

Power struggles are probably the most recognizable form of adult misbehavior. They're the arguments that escalate over nothing—the thermostat, the way the dishwasher is loaded, what time to leave for church. The issue isn't the issue. The issue is control.

Imagine a couple—Michael and Tamara—locked in a cold war over their daughter's school. She wants private education; he says public school is fine. Both make reasonable arguments. But behind Tamara's insistence is a long-standing feeling that Michael never takes her seriously. And behind Michael's resistance is a deeper resentment that he's always overruled. So neither one will budge. Because it's no longer about the school—it's about being heard, being respected, and not being controlled.

Adlerian psychology teaches that *power-driven* misbehavior is a defense mechanism. It's what we do when we feel small. We lash out, not to hurt, but to regain a sense of significance. Dinkmeyer described this goal in *teens* as "the need to feel in charge of one's own life." Adults are no different. We don't want to be dominated. And if we feel our partner is asserting control, we push back.

Sometimes, this looks like direct confrontation. But often, it's subtler—noncompliance, procrastination, silent treatment, stubbornness. A spouse may say, "I'll do it later," knowing full well they won't. Or agree to something and then quietly sabotage it.

The Healthy Response: Don't fight power with more power. That only escalates the conflict. Instead, invite cooperation. Say things like, "Let's figure this out together" or "I want to understand your concerns." Also, create space for each person to make decisions independently when appropriate. Respect breeds mutuality. Control breeds rebellion.

When your partner is fighting for power, resist the urge to "win." Ask instead, "What are they trying to protect? What fear is underneath this?" Empathy disarms power. Collaboration replaces coercion.

3. The Goal of Revenge: "You Hurt Me, So I'll Hurt You Back"

Revenge is rarely announced. It slithers in through back doors: sarcasm, icy stares, pointed silence, emotional withdrawal, public embarrassment. When someone feels deeply hurt—especially repeatedly—they may begin to believe the only way to restore balance is to hurt back.

Think of a man who discovers his wife shared a private issue with her friends. He felt betrayed, humiliated. But rather than express that vulnerability, he becomes sarcastic and sharp in front of her family. He "jokes" about her weight or mocks a decision she made. When she confronts him, he shrugs. "Just playing around."

But it's not a joke. It's revenge.

Adults seeking revenge feel powerless to express their pain constructively. So they attack indirectly. They might withhold affection. Or begin emotionally investing elsewhere—not necessarily in an affair, but in a friendship or hobby that becomes a fortress of avoidance.

The worst part? Revenge behavior breeds more revenge. The hurt partner retaliates. The hostility compounds. Trust deteriorates. And soon, neither person remembers what started the war—only that they're at war.

The Healthy Response: Revenge must be met with compassion and boundaries. Not enabling, but understanding. When a partner lashes out, the question isn't "How dare you?" but "Where are you hurt?" Create safe space for honest conversations. Say, "I feel like you're angry, but I'm not sure why. I care about you, and I want to understand."

And if you're the one feeling vengeful? Stop. Reflect. Ask yourself, "What pain am I avoiding?" Then risk vulnerability. Say, "What you did really hurt me, and I didn't know how to talk about it."

Forgiveness is the only cure for revenge. But forgiveness doesn't mean forgetting or excusing. It means choosing not to weaponize the wound. And that begins with acknowledging it.

4. The Goal of Inadequacy: "I Can't, So I Won't"

The last goal of misbehavior is perhaps the most misunderstood. In children, it shows up as learned helplessness—"I can't do it, so I won't try." In adults, it becomes emotional withdrawal, chronic avoidance, passivity, and sometimes even depression.

Imagine a woman whose husband often points out her faults—how she spends, how she parents, how she organizes the house. Over time, she stops trying. "Nothing I do is good enough," she thinks. "So why bother?" She begins to detach. She forgets things. She becomes apathetic. Her misbehavior isn't defiance—it's despair.

People acting from inadequacy believe they are fundamentally incapable of doing or being enough. So they protect themselves by disengaging. They stop participating in the relationship meaningfully. And sadly, this often provokes more criticism, which deepens their despair. It's a self-fulfilling prophecy.

Or think of a man whose wife has taken on the spiritual leadership of the home because he's reluctant. She pushes. He retreats. She calls him "checked out." He shrugs. In reality, he feels unqualified. So he escapes to video games or work or silence.

The Healthy Response: Affirm competence. Start small. Give your partner space to succeed again—emotionally, spiritually, practically. Say, "I know that didn't go how we hoped, but I see how hard you're trying." Stop rescuing or overcorrecting. Encourage without pressure.

If you're the one in this space, admit the fear. "I'm scared to try because I don't want to fail." Let your partner in. Sometimes, the bravest thing you can do is to start again, even if your knees shake.

Using the Four Diagnostic Questions to Understand Adult Misbehavior

As we've explored the four goals of misbehavior—attention, power, revenge, and inadequacy—it's vital to move from understanding the theory to applying it in the moment, especially when tensions run high. How do you know *which* goal is driving your spouse's (or your own) misbehavior? This is where Dinkmeyer and McKay's

Systematic Training for Effective Parenting of Teens offers one of its most valuable tools: the Four Diagnostic Questions.

Though designed originally for parenting adolescents, these questions are just as effective when dealing with adult misbehavior—particularly in emotionally intimate contexts like marriage. And the beauty of the method is that it doesn't require you to psychoanalyze your partner; it just requires you to pay attention to how you feel in the moment.

Here's how it works:

When you're on the receiving end of a hurtful or confusing behavior, pause and ask yourself:

1. How do I *feel* right now?
2. What am I tempted to do in response?
3. What is my partner really aiming for?
4. What would happen if I responded calmly and differently than I usually do?

Let's break this down with examples for each misbehavior goal.

Misbehavior Goal: Attention

How you feel: Irritated. Annoyed. Drained. Like your time and energy are being consumed by petty demands or constant interruptions.

What you're tempted to do: Scold. Nag. Ignore. Lecture. Maybe give a short burst of attention just to make the behavior stop.

What's really going on: Your partner is craving affirmation and visibility. They're not trying to be obnoxious—they're trying not to disappear.

What works: Choose *proactive connection* over reactive correction. Give positive attention for positive behaviors—before the misbehavior starts. When attention-seeking behavior occurs, respond calmly but don't feed the behavior. Instead, later invite meaningful connection: "I've noticed you've seemed a little off lately. Want to take a walk with me?"

Misbehavior Goal: Power

How you feel: Challenged. Provoked. Like you're being tested or manipulated. You may feel your authority or intelligence is being questioned.

What you're tempted to do: Argue. Insist. Lay down ultimatums. Get loud or passive-aggressive to "win."

What's really going on: Your partner feels insignificant or controlled and is asserting themselves to regain dignity.

What works: *Avoid the power struggle.* Don't fight fire with fire. Offer choices instead of commands. Say, "Here's what I'd like us to work on—how do you think we can make this fair for both of us?" Make room for autonomy within structure. Validate their input even if you ultimately must lead.

Misbehavior Goal: Revenge

How you feel: Hurt. Shocked. Betrayed. You may feel angry but also deeply wounded, as if the behavior was intended to strike you emotionally.

What you're tempted to do: Retaliate. Withdraw emotionally. Say things you'll regret. Return pain for pain.

What's really going on: Your partner feels wronged or unloved and is trying to make you feel what they felt.

What works: Don't retaliate. Instead, respond with *calm empathy*. Say, "That really hurt—and I wonder if you're hurting too. I want to understand." Offer an olive branch without excusing the offense. Restore trust gradually through *forgiveness and safe vulnerability*.

Misbehavior Goal: Inadequacy

How you feel: Hopeless. Frustrated. Exasperated. Like nothing you say or do gets through. You might even feel like giving up.

What you're tempted to do: Take over. Do things yourself. Criticize. Give pep talks. Or just give up.

What's really going on: Your partner feels defeated or incapable and has resigned to failure as a way of self-protection.

What works: Express encouragement without pressure. Offer small, achievable tasks. Celebrate effort over results. Say things like, "I know this has been hard, and I believe in you. Let's take one small step together."

A Real-World Scenario Using the Four Questions

Let's say your partner has been "forgetting" to do something important—pay a bill, call a repairman, or follow through on something they committed to.

You feel *annoyed* (Question 1).

You're tempted to snap or do it yourself (Question 2).

So you ask: Is this about attention? Power? Revenge? Or inadequacy? (Question 3).

- If you feel like they're trying to get a rise out of you, or make you prove how much you care—maybe it's *attention*.
- If you feel they're resisting you just to push back—*power*.
- If it seems they're trying to punish you for something—*revenge*.
- If they seem frozen, depressed, or defeated—*inadequacy*.

Ask yourself: What if I responded differently than I usually do? (Question 4).

Maybe instead of sarcasm, you offer partnership: "I noticed you didn't get to that thing—we all have off days. Want to tackle it together?"

That change of tone doesn't just defuse the situation. It reframes the entire emotional pattern of the relationship.

Why This Matters in Marriage

Most adult conflicts are not about the issue on the surface. They are about unmet needs, misread intentions, and unspoken fears. Using the four questions allows us to *slow down the emotional reaction* and *read the room through a psychological lens*. Instead of punishing the misbehavior, we respond to the need beneath it.

And this is not about enabling dysfunction. It's about discipling one another in love. It's about saying, "I see you acting out, and I'm not going to shame you for it. But I also won't let it slide. I want to know what you really need."

Marriages fall apart not because people change, but because they stop trying to *understand* each other. The Four Questions are a tool to rebuild that understanding—moment by moment, misbehavior by misbehavior, into compassion, trust, and unity.

Final Thought: Misbehavior as a Mirror

Here's the hardest truth of all: these Four Goals aren't just for identifying your partner's misbehavior. They're for identifying your own.

That sarcastic comment? That cold shoulder? That stubborn refusal to give in during an argument? These behaviors have goals, too. And if you're willing to be honest, you'll start catching yourself in the act. You'll start asking, "Am I just trying to win? Am I punishing her for what she said yesterday? Am I withdrawing because I feel like I'll never measure up?"

This doesn't make you bad. It makes you human. And it also makes you capable of change.

So start there. Next time conflict flares, ask the four questions. Not to judge. Not to fix. But to *see*. To see your partner, and yourself, as people who are always trying—clumsily, maybe even painfully—to meet deep emotional needs.

And then respond not with reaction, but with grace. Because when you understand the goal of misbehavior, you can offer the gift every heart longs for: recognition, safety, healing.

That's the beginning of real connection. That's the path back to trust.

Navigating Narcissistic Behavior Through the Lens of Adlerian Psychology

Up to this point, we've explored how misbehavior in relationships often stems from unmet emotional needs—attention, power, revenge, or inadequacy. And for most couples, the misbehavior is *situational*—that is, it emerges under stress, during seasons of disconnection, or as a response to unresolved hurt.

But what happens when misbehavior is *chronic*? What if the pattern isn't occasional or circumstantial—but a consistent way of relating that distorts reality, avoids accountability, and cycles through emotional manipulation? In short: What if you're in a relationship with someone who exhibits narcissistic behavior?

Let's begin by making a critical distinction. We're not talking about clinical narcissistic personality disorder (NPD) as diagnosed in the DSM-5. That requires professional evaluation. What we're addressing here is narcissistic behavior patterns—the kind of relational dysfunction characterized by grandiosity, entitlement, a lack of empathy, constant need for admiration, and an inability or refusal to take responsibility for harm caused. People with narcissistic tendencies often use sophisticated versions of the same misbehavior goals we've already discussed—but in more extreme, entrenched, and manipulative ways. Let's walk through what that looks like through the Adlerian framework and how the Four Questions can help you respond wisely.

When Attention Becomes Narcissistic Supply

In ordinary relationships, the goal of attention is about connection—"see me, notice me." But for someone with narcissistic traits, attention becomes narcissistic supply—a bottomless demand for affirmation, admiration, and praise. It's not just "see me," it's "worship me," and "if you don't, I'll find someone who will." The partner of a narcissist may feel constantly drained, as if they are on emotional call 24/7, needing to validate, admire, and orbit around the narcissist's ego. If that attention dips, they may be punished with coldness, withdrawal, or sudden rage. Often, they're made to feel selfish for wanting space or autonomy.

Your diagnostic cue (Four Questions):

- *How do I feel?* Like I'm walking on eggshells, performing to keep peace.
- *What am I tempted to do?* Give in. Over-affirm. Stay quiet to avoid an explosion.
- *What would work?* Boundaries. Affirm selectively, but refuse to play the role of emotional servant.

Response Tip: Set limits on how much emotional energy you give. You can say, "I care about you, but I can't meet that need in this way right now." Learn the difference between healthy empathy and emotional enmeshment.

When Power Becomes Domination. All humans want agency, but narcissists often crave control. Not just over decisions, but over *narratives*—how the relationship is seen, who is right, and who gets blamed. When challenged, they may escalate into rage, stonewalling, or even gaslighting. They don't just resist being wrong—they rewrite history to ensure they never are. In this dynamic, you may feel controlled, constantly second-guessing your memory or decisions. You may be criticized for asserting yourself, accused of overreacting, or punished with withdrawal or belittling.

Your diagnostic cue (Four Questions):

- *How do I feel?* Invalidated. Dismissed. Silenced.
- *What am I tempted to do?* Fight back, prove my case, or retreat completely.
- *What would work?* Don't engage in power struggles. Set non-negotiable boundaries and protect your mental clarity.

Response Tip: Instead of arguing facts, ground yourself in emotional truth: "I don't feel safe when I'm dismissed like that. This isn't up for debate." Learn to disengage when manipulation arises.

When Revenge Becomes Emotional Abuse. Revenge, when taken to the extreme, becomes punitive in narcissistic relationships. If the narcissistic partner feels slighted—real or imagined—they may retaliate with passive aggression, sabotage, humiliation, or intentional neglect.

They may expose private moments, mock your vulnerabilities, or withhold affection strategically. The message is: *"You hurt me, so I will make you pay. And I will define what 'hurt me' means."*

This creates a relationship built on fear and confusion, where the non-narcissistic partner is constantly managing the fallout of unspoken rules and punishments.

Your diagnostic cue (Four Questions):

- *How do I feel?* **Punished.** Unsafe. Constantly on trial.
- *What am I tempted to do?* Apologize unnecessarily, justify, or retaliate.
- *What would work?* Detach emotionally. Refuse to play the guilt game.

Response Tip: Don't negotiate with vengeance. Call out the pattern: "This feels retaliatory. I won't continue in this conversation if it becomes about punishing me." Have a clear exit strategy when things escalate.

When Inadequacy Becomes Victimhood. Narcissistic individuals rarely own failure. But when they do, it's often through exaggerated inadequacy that manipulates rather than reveals. "I guess I'm just a terrible partner. Nothing I do is ever good enough." This isn't real vulnerability—it's emotional blackmail. They're not sharing to connect—they're collapsing to control the conversation.

You may find yourself constantly trying to reassure them, fix their mood, or rescue them from accountability. Over time, their self-pity shifts the blame back to you: "If I'm this bad, why are you still here? Maybe you're the problem."

Your diagnostic cue (Four Questions):

- *How do I feel?* Guilty. Drained. Manipulated into taking the blame.
- *What am I tempted to do?* Reassure endlessly, or retreat.
- *What would work?* Recognize the emotional bait. Respond with firm compassion.

Response Tip: Don't chase them into the pit. Say, "I hear that you're feeling low. I'll support you when you're ready to take responsibility and move forward. But I won't let this become a spiral."

When Misbehavior Becomes a System. The danger with narcissistic behavior is that it's not occasional—it's systemic. It forms a relational ecosystem where the partner of the narcissist becomes hypervigilant, depleted, and chronically unsure of themselves.

You may start to wonder, "Am I the one misbehaving?" You question your reactions, your needs, your memories. That's the point of narcissistic misbehavior—to create confusion, not clarity. To dominate the emotional airspace so you stop asking for your needs to be met.

So what do you do?

1. Reclaim your clarity. Use the Four Questions not just to understand *them* but to stay anchored in *you*. How do *you* feel? What's *your* healthy response?
2. Set limits—not just with words, but with actions. If you set a boundary and it's trampled, withdraw your participation, attention, or presence accordingly.

3. Stop seeking accountability from someone who can't give it. Focus instead on creating safety and health for yourself.
4. Seek outside help. Whether through therapy, pastoral counsel, or a trusted circle, isolation is the narcissist's greatest weapon. Don't stay alone in confusion.

Discernment with Compassion

Not every difficult person is narcissistic. And not every narcissist is beyond growth. But discernment is critical. Some relationships are simply unhealthy. Others are unsafe. And wisdom from above—"pure, peaceable, gentle, open to reason…" (James 3:17)—requires that we walk in both grace and truth. Remember, you are not called to be consumed by someone else's needs. Love doesn't mean erasure. Patience doesn't mean enabling. Jesus never sacrificed truth to preserve *false peace*. So whether you're dealing with attention-hungry behavior, controlling patterns, emotional retaliation, or manipulative despair, the goal remains the same: respond with clarity, not confusion. With grace, not enabling. With courage, not fear. Let the Four Questions guide you back to solid ground. Let the truth set you free—even when love requires boundaries. And remember: you cannot heal someone by letting them hurt you indefinitely.

When the Ghosts Speak Loudest: Misbehavior Rooted in Past Relationship Wounds

There's a peculiar thing we humans do with pain: if we don't *face it*, we *recreate it*. We bring our unhealed wounds into new relationships, often unconsciously seeking to resolve or relive old stories with new people. Sometimes, we're trying to win battles we lost with our parents. Other times, we're punishing our current partner for a betrayal committed by someone from our past. The details vary, but the dynamic is universal: unresolved emotional injuries have a way of scripting current misbehavior.

This is where Adlerian psychology shines. The Four Goals of Misbehavior are not just about conflict in the moment — they're also the emotional shortcuts we use when we haven't dealt with the long road of healing. Let's explore how each of these goals shows up in a person trying to navigate a *new* relationship while still wounded from an *old* one.

1. Attention: "If You Don't Notice Me, You'll Hurt Me Too"

People who were ignored, dismissed, or neglected in past relationships often enter new ones with a hypersensitive radar for rejection. They might *over-communicate*, constantly ask for reassurance, or *test* the relationship by creating small dramas, just to make sure the other person still cares. It's not manipulation—it's preemptive pain management. "If I can make you notice me now, I won't be blindsided later when you stop loving me like the last person did." But of course, this often backfires. The new partner starts to feel overwhelmed, manipulated, or exhausted. The behavior that was supposed to *prevent abandonment* ends up *provoking it*.

Internal shift needed: Realize that the need for attention is not wrong—but the strategy being used is rooted in fear, not faith. The false belief if that they are not lovable, and are demanding that you, or someone, provides attention in that very moment to prove their worth and assuage their fear. Begin asking, *"Am they asking for care, or are they trying to prevent or mitigate pain? How can you help them to accept and trust your love, rather than to test it? What actions are you taking or have you taken that support their fear, or help them change their perception?"* Remember, you get more of whatever you reward. So, if you reward their demand for caretaking or attendance when it is inappropriate, they will continue to rely upon you for that remedy. Instead, find healthy and appropriate ways to show them they are loveable when they are not demanding it, and do so with frequent regularity, but not when it is demanded. This will help them by rewarding only appropriate non-attention seeking behaviors.

2. Power: "No One Will Ever Control Me Again"

If a previous relationship was marked by dominance, betrayal, or emotional manipulation, the natural reaction is to swing hard in the other direction: Control everything. Refuse to be vulnerable. Be the one with the upper hand. Make no compromises.

This plays out subtly in relationships through ultimatums, inflexibility, or defensiveness. A person who once had their trust violated may now resist any leadership, decision-making, or direction from their new partner—even if it's healthy—because it *feels* like surrender. For example, a man whose ex-wife used financial dependence to control him might now insist on separate everything—separate finances, separate schedules, separate emotional lives. But instead of safety, it creates isolation. The need to stay in control slowly erodes intimacy.

Internal shift needed: Ask yourself, "Is your partner protecting their self from the past, or participating in the present?" Power struggles in new relationships often indicate a loyalty to old wounds. Healing begins when individuals allow someone to contribute without interpreting it as a threat.

3. Revenge: "I'll Make You Pay for What They Did"

This one is difficult to admit—no one wants to believe they're punishing someone who hasn't wronged them. But unresolved betrayal often shows up as retribution aimed at the next person who gets close.

It sounds like sarcasm, dismissiveness, or sharp criticism. Or it might look like withdrawal, avoidance, or even subtle sabotage of the relationship. A part of you *wants* them to fail you—just to validate your pain.

For example, a woman who was cheated on might accuse her faithful boyfriend of being dishonest. She doesn't believe it rationally, but she's emotionally primed to expect betrayal. Her misbehavior is an emotional shield: "If I assume the worst, I'll never be surprised again." But that protection also prevents connection. The heart says, "I won't be a victim again," but in doing so, it becomes a punisher.

Internal shift needed: Ask, *"Does my partner really see me clearly, or through the lens of someone who hurt them?"* The current partner is not the past one. But when viewing them as the same, it *resurrects the old wounds* instead of redeeming them.

Pain must be expressed to be healed, rather than projecting onto others.

4. Inadequacy: "I'm Broken, and You'll Leave Me Too"

Some people don't fight, don't sabotage, don't criticize—they simply *collapse*. They come into a new relationship already defeated, convinced they're too much, not enough, or unworthy. Maybe they were constantly criticized by a parent or ex-partner. Maybe they were told they'd never change or never measure up. Now, even in a relationship full of grace, they live like they're on borrowed time.

Example: A man who was repeatedly told by his ex-wife that he was a failure might now interpret every suggestion from his new girlfriend as criticism. When she says, "Let's try doing the budget this way," he hears, "You're not good enough." His response? Shut down. Stop trying. Emotionally disengage. This isn't laziness—it's a defense mechanism. "If I don't try, I can't fail. If I don't engage, I can't be rejected."

Internal shift needed: The first step is naming the wound: "I was made to feel inadequate, but that doesn't mean I am." You or your partner need to risk re-engagement. Healing doesn't come from waiting to feel worthy—it comes from acting in trust despite the fear.

The Redemptive Opportunity: Turning Misbehavior Into Healing

Here's the great irony: The misbehavior that creates relational dysfunction is often driven by a *desire for healing*. People are not just lashing out. They are trying to rewrite the script. They are hoping that if this time someone loves them *through* their worst moments, the pain will finally go away. And that's not entirely wrong. God often heals us through relationships. But not when we reenact old wounds blindly. Healing begins when we name the pattern and choose a different path. This is where Dinkmeyer's Four Questions become a tool of transformation. If you find that you are the one who is projecting or acting out, you can use them on yourself:

1. **How do *I* feel right now?**
2. (Am I scared? Ashamed? Needy? Defensive?)
3. **What am *I* tempted to do?**
4. (Withdraw? Attack? Manipulate? Collapse?)
5. What might *I really* be needing or fearing?
6. (Validation? Control? Safety? Worth?)
7. **What would it look like to respond *differently* this time?**
8. (Could I name my fear instead of masking it? Could I ask for help without guilt?)

When you do this, you move from reaction to redemption. From repeating the story to *rewriting it*.

You're Allowed to Begin Again

If you've seen your partner or yourself in these patterns, it does not mean that either of you are necessarily broken. You're human. You've loved, you've been hurt, and you've developed strategies to survive. But survival is not the same as healing. And God has not called you merely to survive your past—but to *heal through it* and *love beyond it*. That begins by seeing **misbehavior** for what it really is: a signal. A clue. A coded message saying, **"Something still hurts. Please handle with care."**

You don't have to fix it all today. You don't have to be perfect before you're loved. But you do have to be honest. You do have to take responsibility—not for the pain inflicted on you, but for the patterns it left behind. And with that responsibility comes something powerful: the ability to choose differently. To respond in truth. To love more wisely. To grow beyond your wounds. You are not your misbehavior. You are not your past. You are not your worst day.

You are someone who is *learning how to walk in the light of grace*—even if you limp a little on the way.

Misbehavior Is a Message — So Learn Its Language

Every relationship tells a story—but not always the one we think we're writing. Underneath every sharp word, every cold shoulder, every silent treatment or explosive reaction is a message. A coded cry. A signal flare rising from someone who, whether they know it or not, is saying: *"Please understand me, even when I don't know how to ask."*

Adler's genius was his insistence that behavior is purposeful—even when it's dysfunctional. The late-night argument, the passive-aggressive silence, the sarcastic jab, the withdrawn partner who seems checked out—none of it is random. None of it is senseless. It may be immature, it may be destructive, it may even be deeply painful—but it's almost always an attempt to meet a need.

That's what the Four Goals of Misbehavior teach us. And what Dinkmeyer's Four Questions help us do is decipher the moment—to go beneath reaction, beneath blame, beneath our own frustration and ask:

- How do I feel right now?
- What am I tempted to do in response?
- What goal might be driving their (or my) behavior?
- What would happen if I responded differently than I usually do?

When used with humility and discernment, these questions become a relational superpower. They move us from defensiveness to curiosity, from reactivity to responsibility. They help us *see the person behind the behavior*, and respond not just with firmness, but with grace.

But we must also acknowledge that not every relationship conflict is created equal. Sometimes, misbehavior is chronic and entrenched—not the occasional dysfunction of a tired spouse or the outburst of an overwhelmed parent, but a systemic pattern of emotional domination, manipulation, or gaslighting. That's the realm of narcissistic behavior. And when you're on the receiving end of that cycle—where attention is demanded, power is seized, vengeance is subtle but relentless, and victimhood is weaponized—you begin to lose your sense of self.

In those relationships, the *Four Questions* aren't just a tool to understand *them*. They're a lifeline to remember *you*. They help you discern what's real, what's yours to own, and what isn't. They teach you how to engage without enabling, how to set limits without apology, and how to protect your peace without guilt. Still other times, the misbehavior in front of you isn't even about you—it's about someone else's *unfinished story*. A person wounded by betrayal may test your loyalty. Someone who was controlled in a former relationship may resist even your healthy leadership. A partner who was criticized for years may now recoil at your gentle feedback, assuming it's another attack. Here, misbehavior isn't malicious—it's protective. They're not trying to punish you—they're trying to preempt more pain. But without self-awareness, that strategy poisons the very intimacy they long to preserve.

And again, the Four Questions serve you. Not just to analyze them, but to examine yourself. Because the truth is, we all bring baggage. We all misbehave sometimes. We all feel small or afraid or inadequate. The question isn't *if* you will act out—but *whether* you will recognize it in time to change your course. So here's where we land, full circle: Attention says, *"Do I matter?" Power says, *"Will you respect me?"* Revenge says, *"Do you know how much you hurt me?"* Inadequacy says, *"Am I enough?"*

And when you begin to see misbehavior through that lens—not just as something to stop, but something to understand—you unlock a whole new path in your relationships. One marked not by control or fear, but by *compassion and clarity*. This doesn't mean tolerating abuse. It doesn't mean making excuses. It means committing to see people, and yourself, as more than the moment. It means becoming a translator of pain—not to absorb it, but to *transform it*. It means saying, in essence: "I won't let this behavior define us. I won't be manipulated by it. But I also won't reduce you to it. I'll respond in a new way, because I'm not just here to win—I'm here to love wisely." That's what maturity looks like. Not perfect behavior. But understood behavior, handled with courage.

So let this be your resolve, to slow down enough to ask the four questions. To dig deep enough to see the root. To stand strong enough to set the boundary. To love well enough to risk a new response. You are not at the mercy of misbehavior—yours or anyone else's. You have the tools to respond with strength, the wisdom to interpret the message, and the Spirit of God to guide you. Because in the end, misbehavior is not the enemy. *Misunderstanding is.* And understanding—that sacred, stubborn, redemptive kind—might just be what your relationship needs most.

Field Notes:

1. Situation Report:

Where did this chapter hit home for me?

2. Operational Insight:

What truth or principle stands out to me the most?

3. Action Step:

What's one small thing I will do differently this week because of this chapter?

4. Words to Say:

Who needs to hear something from me?

5. Brief Prayer:

Write a one-sentence prayer asking God to strengthen your character in this area.

Carrying the Banner
You Are on Display

A Banner Life

There's a moment that catches most men off guard—not because it's loud, but because it's quiet. It happens between emails. In the driveway. Over a sink of dishes or in the stillness of an early morning before anyone else is awake.

It's that flash of realization: I've built something... but what does it mean?

You start to look at your marriage, your kids, your habits, and wonder: *Is the man they see the man I think I am?*

Here's the truth: you are always flying a flag. Whether you're aware of it or not, your life is waving a banner that tells your family, your friends, your coworkers—and your God—*what kingdom you represent.* The only question is: whose name is on it?

You don't get to live like a free agent when you belong to Christ. The moment you take on His name—Christian—you've declared allegiance. You've picked up a banner. And the world is watching what it says.

The Command We Keep Misunderstanding

"You shall not take the name of the Lord your God in vain."

Most Christian men interpret this as "Don't swear using God's name." But that's only the surface. The deeper, heavier meaning of this commandment is not about profanity—it's about identity.

To "take the name of the Lord" is to *carry it*, to adopt it, to represent it.

To take that name "in vain" is to misrepresent it. To wear His title but not reflect His character. To walk under the banner of Jesus while advancing the kingdom of self. To claim loyalty to Christ while living as if your preferences and priorities are the highest authority.

You can violate this commandment every single day—without ever cursing.

If you call yourself a Christian husband but treat your wife like a burden instead of a blessing, you take His name in vain. If you call yourself a spiritual leader but use Scripture to justify selfishness, you take His name in vain. If your kids see "God" as a word you use but not a life you live, you take His name in vain.

It is not your *intentions* that define you. It is your *representation*.

Marriage: A Spiritual, Not Social, Contract

God didn't design marriage as a lifestyle upgrade. He ordained it as a **living typology**—a sacred model of His redemptive plan.

Marriage is:

A **biological alliance**, binding bodies and generations.

A **psychological alliance**, meeting needs and fostering healing.

A **cultural alliance**, building legacy and tradition.

But above all, a **spiritual alliance**, representing Christ and the Church.

In marriage, God calls the man to **model Christ's love**—not in sentiment, but in *sacrifice*. To lay down his glory, his pride, his comfort—for the sake of his wife.

When a man takes on this role but refuses this posture, he becomes a contradiction. He takes on the image of Christ but lives for the image of self.

Vignette: The Banner Over Breakfast

I once sat across the table from a man named David—a successful entrepreneur, church deacon, two-time Ironman finisher. From the outside, he looked like the model Christian man. Sharp suit. Polished speech. Beautiful family. Sunday church regular. The type of guy other men admire and wives say, "Why can't you be more like him?"

But as he stirred cream into his coffee, his gaze dropped low, and he said softly, "I think my wife doesn't like me. I think my kids respect me—but they don't know me. And I think I've been leading my home more like a CEO than a servant."

It wasn't said in bitterness. It was said in revelation.

He paused, then looked up again. "Honestly, I've realized that my family got swallowed up in my identity. The identity I built in the marketplace, at church, in the community... all that has bled into my home. My drive. My expectations. My metrics. Somewhere along the way, I used my Christianity as a way to build credibility—not character. I wore the label to earn trust and advantage. To get favor with clients, to seem like the safe guy in social spaces. I used it to elevate myself. But I never let it **transform me**."

Silence lingered between us. He wasn't confessing sin as much as he was discovering it. His thoughts were still forming, but the truth was already pressing in.

He continued, voice tight. "I've been wondering lately—if my kids respect me, what for? Because I make money? Because I've given them a good life? Because I've kept things orderly? Or is it something deeper? Do they see a man they want to become, or just a man who knows how to win?"

He looked back down. "If they could see my heart... what would they actually see? What would *I* see?"

And then, the deepest question: "What does God already see?"

The table between us felt heavy. Not with shame, but with sacred clarity. David had carried the banner of success. The banner of Christian culture. The banner of competence.

But he had not been carrying the banner of Christ.

He had called himself a believer, a family man, a leader—but he had led in a way that elevated himself and kept others at arm's length. He had *presented* Jesus, but not *embodied* Him. His Christian identity had become a **facade**—a set of values to display, not a heart to be conformed.

And now, with everything intact on paper—retirement funded, reputation pristine, family photos smiling—he felt the ache of a man who had climbed the wrong mountain with a Jesus sticker on his gear.

David realized that the banner he had been flying over his home said: "Efficient. Controlled. Successful." But not "Christ-like."

He hadn't been abusive. He hadn't been immoral. But he had been **absent in the way that mattered most**: emotionally, spiritually, and relationally.

And now, the question that mattered more than the balance in his accounts or the accomplishments on his resume was this: **Was he representing the name he claimed—or misusing it?** Had he taken the Lord's name in vain—not with profanity, but with *hollow presence*?

That morning, David didn't vow to work less or do more devotionals. He just sat there, quiet, reckoning with the gap between the **man he said he was** and the **man he truly reflected**.

And in that stillness, the Spirit did what only He can do— He began to gently strip the false banners, so a real one could be raised.

David's moment was not a failure. It was a grace. A revealing. Because sometimes God lets a man's image shatter so that his identity can finally take root. Some men wake up to their own hollowness. Others are gently exposed by those closest to them—wives who feel more like props than partners, children who grow up in houses run like organizations instead of homes built on love. Mark was one of those men.

The Sermon She Heard

There's a man I counseled years ago—Mark—a faithful churchgoer, small group leader, and respected elder. On paper, he was every bit the spiritual leader. He tithed generously, knew his Bible, and had even led a marriage seminar once. But his wife came to me first.

"I know he loves God," she said, eyes cast downward. "But I feel more like a ministry partner than a wife. I feel like we're running a Christian operation instead of sharing a life. He doesn't yell. He's not mean. He's...efficient."

She hesitated, then looked up with tears forming. "He quotes Scripture. But I feel like furniture. I know he's a good man. But I don't feel loved—I feel *managed*."

When Mark finally came in, it was clear he had no idea.

"I thought things were fine," he said. "I mean, I work hard, I lead devotions, I've never been unfaithful. What else does she want?"

She didn't want *more* of him. She wanted a *different him*. One that didn't just teach about Christ, but who *looked like Christ*—in how he listened, touched, responded, repented.

Mark hadn't been cruel. But he had been **calculating**. He had measured spiritual success the same way he measured metrics at work—by inputs and outcomes. What he missed was that his wife didn't want performance. She wanted **presence**.

The sermon of his life had preached Christ with *doctrine*, but not with *demeanor*. And while his theology was precise, his tone was distant. The result? His wife heard a gospel that sounded like pressure, not peace.

Mark hadn't misrepresented Jesus with sin. He had done it with silence. With efficiency. With emotional distance. He had taken the name of the Lord in vain—not loudly, but subtly. And in doing so, the sermon she heard was this: **Christ is efficient. Christ gets things done. Christ provides. But Christ doesn't feel.** And slowly, painfully, she stopped believing that love was more than a task to complete. She didn't want **more**. She wanted **real**. Not religious efficiency, but spiritual *intimacy*.

Mark had unintentionally preached a distorted gospel in his home—one where God was busy, structured, distant. His theology was sharp. His love was dull. **Leadership without emotional presence is not love—it's administration. And his home didn't need a manager. It needed a man who mirrored Christ.**

The Quiet Drift of Disappointment

Sometimes a wife doesn't protest—she just grows silent. Not in bitterness, but in resignation. That's what happened in James' home.

When She Stopped Smiling

James had been married twelve years when it happened—quietly, almost imperceptibly. He walked in the door after work and noticed his wife didn't look up. She didn't smile. No warm greeting. No hello. Just... silence. At first, he chalked it up to stress. Maybe the kids had been hard. Maybe she was tired. A few days went by, and the same thing happened again. Eventually, on a rare quiet night after the kids were down, he asked, "Is everything okay? You've been really... distant."

She looked at him, not coldly, but with a kind of gentle exhaustion. "I stopped smiling," she said softly, "because I stopped hoping." She wasn't angry. She wasn't dramatic. She was empty. And James realized something terrifying: he had slowly become a man who **no longer stirred her hope**. Those five words shattered him.

They weren't fighting. He wasn't neglectful in the obvious ways. The bills were paid. The home was stable. The schedule ran like a machine. But somewhere in the rhythm of doing life, James had stopped loving her with *joy*. With pursuit. With intention. She didn't feel chosen—she felt **stuck**. And she wasn't blaming him—she was revealing him. He realized that for years, he'd been carrying the banner of responsibility. Of provision. Of "solid guy." He had been trying so hard to be a *good man*, he forgot to be a *present husband*. And as he lay in bed that night staring at the ceiling, he asked himself the same question David had once asked: **If my wife could see my heart—what would she see?** Would she see warmth? Compassion? Sacrifice? Or would she see a man who quietly resented the demands of love? James saw it clearly now: he had taken the Lord's name and used it to prop up a sanitized version of manhood—strong, stable, respected. But not *Christ-like*. And in the absence of his emotional presence, her heart had grown quiet.

He realized that he had confused *being a good man* with *being a Christ-like husband*. Provision is not the same as pursuit. Proximity is not the same as presence. And faithfulness is not just staying—it's staying engaged.

When Conviction Isn't Connection

There are men who do all the "right" things and still miss the relational heart of God. Ethan was one of them.

The Man Who Lost the Mirror

Ethan was a man of conviction. He knew what was right and wrong. He taught his sons about honor. He led family prayer. But his wife rarely spoke in those moments. She listened—but with a forced calm, as if sitting through something obligatory. And when Ethan would finish, he'd often leave the room feeling proud—"leading his home," he thought.

What he didn't see was that his leadership came with no invitation. It felt **like a script**—one where everyone else had to recite lines while he delivered the monologue.

His wife, Alana, finally told him one day, "You're a good man, but I don't feel known by you. You ask me to submit—but submit to *what*? A schedule? A standard? I don't feel like I'm walking beside you. I feel like I'm being graded by you."

Ethan was stunned.

He had equated morality with godliness. Discipline with discipleship. But he had lost **the mirror** of empathy. His kids respected him, but they didn't run to him. His wife honored him, but she didn't feel safe with him.

In his attempt to carry the banner of righteousness, Ethan had forgotten to carry the **heart of the King**—the One who knelt before washing feet. Who wept with the grieving. Who embraced lepers.

The Jesus Ethan preached was **true**, but not **tangible**.

Ethan had built a system around his faith—but not a sanctuary. He protected moral boundaries but failed to protect emotional space. **His wife needed Jesus—not in Ethan's statements, but in his posture. And the mirror of leadership revealed a man who looked more like a lecturer than a lover.**

The Ruin and the Reflection Aaron didn't see himself clearly until everything fell apart.

The Man in the Mirror

There was a moment, years after the fallout of his first marriage, when Aaron looked into the mirror and whispered, "I wouldn't want to be married to me either."

It wasn't self-loathing. It was finally seeing what his wife had lived with for years: a man who led out of anxiety, not love. A man who made every spiritual discipline about performance. A man who measured worth by control.

He had called himself "protector," but his tone had been sharp. He had called himself "leader," but his presence had been absent. He had quoted Ephesians 5, but lived Galatians 5:20—fits of rage, selfish ambition, dissension.

He didn't cheat. He didn't abuse. But he had **never submitted to Christ** in a way that formed him into someone *worthy of submission*.

Looking back, Aaron realized: He had flown a flag. It just wasn't God's.

Aaron took God's name—but never surrendered to His heart. And by the time he saw it, he had already lost what mattered most.

The Character That Carries the Banner

What makes a man trustworthy is not his power—but his **predictability**. Not in emotion, but in *virtue*.

Can your wife predict that you will listen with grace? That your tone will reflect patience? That your faith will shape your decisions—not just on Sundays, but in how you respond to irritation, exhaustion, temptation?

To carry the name of Christ is to make **His presence visible** in your most ordinary interactions.

The Banner You Were Born to Bear

You don't have to be spectacular. But you must be **sincere**. You don't have to get it right every time. But you must be *willing to repent when you don't*. The question isn't whether you're leading. You are. The question is whether your leadership reveals the One you claim to follow, or just your own limited self? So ask yourself, what do the people closest to me believe about Jesus because of me? What name am I actually carrying? What kingdom does my life display?

You were not called to impress your family, your friends, your church, or your work peers. You were called to *represent* Christ to them all, and to have a *transformative* effect on them. So raise His banner. Not just in your beliefs—but in your behavior. Let your home feel His love. Let your children see His gentleness. Let your wife feel His pursuit. Let the world see His grace. Because when you carry His name with honor—you don't just lead a life, you reveal a Kingdom.

Field Notes:

1. Situation Report:

Where did this chapter hit home for me?

2. Operational Insight:

What truth or principle stands out to me the most?

3. Action Step:

What's one small thing I will do differently this week because of this chapter?

4. Words to Say:

Who needs to hear something from me?

5. Brief Prayer:

Write a one-sentence prayer asking God to strengthen your character in this area.

Attend to the Tree Not the Fruit

In one of his books, Andy Andrews [2] talks about evidence. He makes a point of saying if you were to find a leaf or a piece of fruit lying on the ground and you could identify it you could be assured that somewhere there was a tree that produced that leaf or that piece of fruit. For instance, if you found an orange on the ground you would have reason to believe that there was an orange tree somewhere. Or if you

---

[2] Andrews, A. (2013). *The noticer returns: Sometimes you find perspective, and sometimes perspective finds you*. Thomas Nelson.

found an orange leaf on the ground it would be evidence that there is an orange tree somewhere. Further, if the orange was a healthy well-developed orange you could infer from that that there was a healthy orange tree that gave birth to that orange. Likewise if there was a diseased unhealthy leaf then there was likely an unhealthy diseased tree somewhere. We can judge by the produce quality of the tree.

So often what I'm dealing with men, or we could just say people, but this book is about men, that they are highly motivated to deal with the produce or the evidence of their life. I call this image maintenance. Men are motivated to massage the image that other people hold in their minds about them. The facade. The belief. The image. I remember when I took my kids to Disneyworld, and we went over to the universal studio lot. You stand on the street that represents a typical movie backlot, and you notice that the buildings look real that are up close to you. But, as the tour guide explains, as you look down the street the street narrows and the buildings become less realistic and eventually, they are painted backgrounds. From the perspective of the camera, they all blend together and look like a long street when really it's a short alley. This is a facade.

We all know that in movies these street scenes are just backdrops. I have one in my recording studio. I change it out periodically. Every once in a while people notice it and they realize it's not real. Other times it looks very real. It doesn't really matter to me because I know it's not real. And it's not intended to be real. It's just a backdrop. But in a movie realism sometimes is important. And for men, the facade is oftentimes the most important thing. But ask yourself why?

Has your growing up as a young man or a boy you learn this all encompassing importance early on. Boys are taught from a young age certain facts, if we can call them that. One of my favorite examples is "big boys don't cry." This is a supposed fact. But of course it is not a fact, it is a bold-faced lie that parents and the rest of the world tell boys from a very young age in order to stop them from crying. This is part of social conditioning. The only fact is that the culture doesn't want boys to cry because the culture is deemed this to be inappropriate for boys. The culture fears that if boys cry then when they become men they will be weak and effective men and society shuns weak and ineffective men.

Therefore the boys must be conditioned early not to cry among other things so that they will be strong effective men. There's no thought given to what this does to the emotional state of little boys. But if you think about it is surely quite damning to a child. After all, if big boys don't cry, but as a little boy I am crying, and I am expected to be a big boy, but I am crying, I must not be a big boy, therefore I'm failing, therefore there's something wrong with me...

You can see how this confuses a child. Especially considering that a child sees himself as the center of the universe naturally so. This egocentrism is part of being a child. So if a little boy is crying but this is somehow damning to a child then this child must be damned. This is part of emotional reasoning. If it feels bad, it must be bad. And if it is bad, and I keep doing it, then I'm bad. And if

I'm bad, then there's something wrong with me. If there's something wrong with me, then people will not like me, therefore I'm unlikeable. If I'm unlikeable, then no one will ever like me, and therefore I will be alone rejected and abandoned. This is the stuff that psychologist make their living off.

So, without getting into all the attachment disorders and narcissistic disorders and all the things that might possibly breed from this, let's just say this about that: boys learn from an early age that what other people think about them matters more than reality. So, they spend a lot of time trying to correct the fruits and produce in their life, I.e., their image. Image maintenance becomes their primary focus. If you don't see it, or if you don't believe you're lying eyes, then it didn't happen.

Plausible deniability is power. If a man can convince someone that what they saw isn't what they saw then he's safe. Deniability. This is a superpower for men. Blame shift, gas lighting, any of the narcissistic resistances make sense to him. This is because these are powerful ways to push off any feelings of inadequacy and shame.

For me as a counselor, one of the most frustrating tasks I have is to explain to wives why shame avoidance is so important to men. I've had women tell me universally that men just need to get over it. They just need to get past it. They just need to stop feeling the shame. They don't understand that men cannot get past it. Man cannot get over it. Man cannot just stop feeling the shame. Their wives do not understand that when they criticize their husbands for something that seems so simple to women, in other words just stop feeling that way. That it triggers a shame to go deeper. And so the women lose patients with the man, the men feel like failures 10 times over, and they go even deeper into the resistance and their need to build a thicker facade. And a perpetuates cycle. For men it's easier to explain. I like to joke with the men, by explaining to them the simplicity of the situation. For men, we know that the fastest way to get a woman mad at them is for them to advise their wives to simply "calm down" and to "just let it go" and to "move on" from whatever is bothering them. These bits of advice seem so simple. Why can't wives just do that? After all, it works for men. Of course, any man that's been married for more than a minute knows that if he was to say one of these three things to his wives he's likely to find a sharp object protruding from his body somewhere. And rightly so. This advice doesn't work for women. It does work for men.

But when a woman tells a man that he needs to stop thinking about himself and stop worrying about his own image and his shame and things like that she is in fact telling him to, "calm down" or two, "just get over himself" or some other similar notion that makes sense to women. It has the same effect on men that it has on women except that men cannot express the deep level of hurt because that then deepens their shame and so they go into an aggressive fight or flight response instead of a emotional response. Which do women makes no sense whatsoever. But if you're a guy reading this book, which is the audience it's written for it's going to make sense to you.

So what do you do as a guy? You start attending to the fruit, the produce. You're trying to correct the blemishes on the fruit. You're trying to polish the apples. You're trying to make the image look good. But this is the mistake. We call this gas lighting for a reason. Or blame shifting. You're trying to take the outcome and make it appear to be something that it's not. Gas lighting is a term that's being bounced around a lot in the current culture. For those who don't know what it is it is a term that actually comes from an old movie. In the movie a man is trying to make his bride believe that she is losing her mind. In order to make her doubt her perceptions he is systematically dimming the gas lights in the house. When she complains that it's darker than normal he denies it. While she sees that the room is darker he keeps denying the evidence. Eventually she doesn't believe her own eyes because he is reflecting back to her that the evidence that she believes is actually faulty. This is an effort to make her believe him not her own perception. This is where we get the term gas lighting. So gas lighting is when someone tries to convince you to believe their story and not your perception. It is an effort to manipulate your understanding contrary to the evidence of reality. When somebody doesn't like reality such as the quality of the produce of their life they often use gas lighting to convince you that the produce is actually better than it is.

Blame shift and gas lighting go together often. Blame shift is simply where the person who has done something untoward, or selfishly, or manipulatively flips the script and makes it your fault. We see this quite often with people who are passive aggressive. They'll say something or do something that it's hard to blame them for yet somehow we know that it's their fault but they've done it in a way that it's hard to point the finger directly at them. In blame shifting the person who actually is responsible has left some plausible deniability, or they just outright say it's your fault. I see this a lot with abusers. A man will get angry at his wife and hit her. And then he'll apologize and say I'm so sorry I hit you but you made me so angry. This is a blame shift. He's acknowledging that he hit her which is wrong. But, he's blaming her for making him angry. The blame shift is if you didn't make me angry I wouldn't have hit you there for it must be your fault. If she allows this line of reasoning to stand, then she is actually excusing him and blaming herself.

You can see that blame shifting and gas lighting tend to go together. Both rely on shifting reality to cause the person being manipulated to doubt their own interpretation of facts. This is polishing the apple with wax to make it look shiny even though the inside is rotten. This is what I mean by attending to the produce or the fruit.

So what's the solution? What we hinted at in the first chapter about popping the hood. Preventative maintenance on a car happens, not when the car breaks down in the middle of the street, but beforehand in little attendances. Changing the oil on a regular basis. Inflating the tires and rotating them. Changing the filters, the spark plugs in the wires, keeping up with inspections. Thanks for that nature. Minor little maintenances which when done, which are not really inconvenient, and not very costly will keep the engine running smoothly for a long time. But when neglected can have a catastrophic and costly outcome.

If you want to have healthy quality oranges on your orange tree you will cultivate your tree not your oranges. You will make sure the ground is healthy and full of nutrients. You will water that ground. You will cultivate the ground. You will make sure that there are no harmful pests or chemicals. You will prune the tree periodically. You will make sure that there are no competitive plants or weeds. You will make sure nothing's blocking the sun. You will shelter the tree if there is going to be a frost. In other words, you'll do preventative maintenance on that tree and give it what it needs. If you do all this you will have a crop of healthy delicious oranges on a regular basis. But if you neglect to do these things you will have stunted spotty sour dry oranges that you will not enjoy. If you were to compare your oranges to somebody else's oranges they would be able to evaluate the state of your tree versus the other person's tree by the fruit. You could try to explain away the differences but you would have to gaslight or blame shift quite a bit.

The lesson here my friend is to attend to the tree not to the fruit. Once the fruit is produced it is done. It has left the tree and inspection is beyond your control. It is what it is. Once you have poisoned the fruit others will see it. If your children resent you for your behavior you cannot undo that. If your wife has been betrayed and harmed by you you cannot undo that. If your boss thinks you're a bad employee you cannot undo that. If the world knows you as an angry person you cannot undo that. In other words the fruit has been produced and you have to accept it. But, if you attend to the tree the fruit that you produce hereafter can be sweet and abundant. And that fruit can change the future. It won't happen overnight. And the fruit that you produced in the past will still be remembered. But the fruit that you produce in the future can become valuable and appreciated. But the choices up to you. Do you want to continue defending the old fruit by gaslighting blame shifting or other pretenses of fruit manipulation? Or would you rather have a produce that you can be proud of and stand behind?

Field Notes:

1. Situation Report:
Where did this chapter hit home for me?

2. Operational Insight:
What truth or principle stands out to me the most?

3. Action Step:
What's one small thing I will do differently this week because of this chapter?

4. Words to Say:
Who needs to hear something from me?

5. Brief Prayer:
Write a one-sentence prayer asking God to strengthen your character in this area.

Fruit From a Poisoned Tree

It began with the well.

No one remembered when the poison first seeped into the water, only that it had always been there, hidden beneath the surface. The well sat at the edge of the land, nestled among the roots of a great tree, a towering oak that had stood longer than anyone could recall. Its branches stretched wide, casting deep shadows over the soil below, its roots digging deep into the earth, drinking from the unseen source.

For years, the tree had been strong. It had withstood storms that tore weaker trees from the ground. It had provided shade in the summer, shelter in the rain, and in the autumn, it bore fruit—small, round, golden-red. But something had changed.

The poison in the water was subtle at first. The tree absorbed it slowly, unknowingly, its roots pulling up what it needed to survive. The leaves, once vibrant, dulled. The bark darkened, cracking in places. Then the fruit came, and it looked the same—beautiful, ripe, full. But when the villagers picked it, when they bit into the soft flesh, they recoiled. The taste was wrong. Worse, those who ate it fell ill. First, a bitter taste on the tongue. Then a deep, aching sickness that spread through their bodies like unseen roots, winding through veins and bone, stealing strength, turning warmth into cold.

Over time, the villagers learned. They stopped coming to the tree. They whispered about it instead. Children were warned never to play beneath its branches. Lovers who once sat in its shade now avoided it. The tree, once beloved, became feared. And so it stood alone, its branches stretching into an empty sky, bearing fruit that no one would eat.

Elena had once been like that tree before the poison took root.

She had been full of life, laughter ringing through the air like the rustling of leaves in a summer breeze. Her heart had been open, her love given freely, without hesitation. She had been someone people turned to—her kindness a well from which others drank.

Then the loss came.

It was not one great tragedy but a slow, creeping sorrow that settled into her bones. The death of her mother. The betrayal of a friend. The love she had given that had not been returned. Each wound another drop of poison in the well of her heart.

At first, it was invisible. She told herself she was fine, that time would heal. But grief is not patient. It does not wait for permission to spread. It seeps into the deepest places, winding through the soul like unseen roots.

She stopped trusting so easily. The warmth in her voice cooled. Smiles became scarce, and when they came, they did not reach her eyes. She told herself she was only protecting herself, but in truth, she was walling herself in.

And then came the fruit.

Her words, once gentle, became sharp. The love she had once given freely was now measured, cautious, laced with bitterness. She spoke, and those who heard her felt the weight of her pain, though they did not always understand its source. Those who stayed close grew weary, poisoned by her resentment, her suspicion, her inability to let go of wounds long past. Some tried to help her, to pull her back from the edge, but grief had become her identity. She clung to it as if letting go meant losing the last pieces of herself.

One by one, people left. Not because they did not care, but because they could not withstand the poison. And so, like the tree, she stood alone.

One autumn afternoon, long after the villagers had stopped coming near the tree, a healer arrived in the village. She was old, with silver hair and steady hands, and she had seen trees like this before. She walked to the well, kneeling beside it, brushing her fingers over the stones.

"The water is poisoned," she said simply.

The villagers nodded. "We know. We stopped drinking from it long ago."

The healer shook her head. "That's not enough. The tree is still drinking."

They hesitated. "It's too late for the tree," one said.

The healer looked up at the withered branches, at the fruit that no one touched. Then she stepped forward, placing a hand against the bark. "Not if we cleanse the source."

And so they did. They dug deep, pulling up the earth around the well, finding the hidden veins of poison, tracing them back to where the water had first turned. They cleared the corruption, letting clean water flow once more. It took time. The tree did not heal overnight.

But season by season, the bark brightened. The leaves grew richer in color. And when the fruit finally came again, the healer took one in her hands, broke it open, and smiled. It was sweet.

Elena stood at the edge of her own poisoned well, staring at the reflection in its dark waters. She saw the lines of sorrow etched into her face, the weight of grief still heavy on her shoulders. And for the first time, she asked herself, **What if I could be healed?**

She had spent years believing that pain was something to be carried, that to release it was to dishonor the loss. But she had not realized how it had seeped into every part of her, how it had turned her heart bitter, how it had pushed away those who had once loved her.

She knelt by the well of her soul and did what she had been afraid to do for so long.

She began to cleanse the source.

It started with a choice—to let go of the past, not because it didn't matter, but because she did. To forgive, not because the pain wasn't real, but because it no longer had to define her. To believe, even if only in the smallest way, that healing was possible.

And like the tree, it would take time.

But one day, when her heart bore fruit again, it would no longer be poison. It would be life.

Alternate Version

Fruit From a Poisoned Tree

It began with the well.

No one knew exactly when the poison first seeped into the water. Perhaps it had always been there, hidden beneath the surface, its presence unnoticed until it was too late. The well sat at the edge of the land, nestled among the roots of a great tree—tall, strong, a fixture of the village.

For years, the tree had been a source of shelter, a place of respite beneath its sprawling branches. It bore fruit each season—round, golden-red, sweet to the taste. The villagers trusted its harvest, relied on its steady gifts.

But something had changed.

The poison in the water came slow, unseen. The tree drank deeply, never questioning the source that had always sustained it. The leaves dulled. The bark cracked, darkened. Then the fruit came, and outwardly, it looked the same—beautiful, full, promising. But those who ate it recoiled. The sweetness was gone, replaced by something bitter, something that burned the tongue. And worse—those who swallowed it grew sick.

At first, the villagers didn't understand. They kept coming, believing the next fruit would be different. But time revealed the truth: the poison had reached the heart of the tree. What had once been a source of life was now a source of sickness. And so, the villagers stayed away.

The tree remained, standing tall and alone, bearing fruit that no one would eat.

Elena had once been like that tree.

She had been full of life, full of love, her heart wide open to the man who had promised to cherish it. When she and Daniel married, she believed she had found her forever—someone who would walk beside her, stand with her, hold her close through every season of life.

And then came the betrayal.

It wasn't something she saw coming. The truth had unraveled slowly, like a thread pulled loose from a seam, until suddenly, her world was undone. She didn't know what was worse—the fact that he had done it, or the fact that he still said he loved her. That he wanted to stay.

She had stayed, too. At least, physically.

But deep within her, something had changed.

Anger seeped into her, settled in the hidden places of her heart. At first, it gave her strength. It kept her standing when grief threatened to pull her under. It gave her clarity, focus—a fire to keep from feeling the full weight of the hurt.

But anger, like poison, does not stay contained.

Over time, it wound through her, tainting everything it touched. She stopped seeing Daniel as the man she had once loved; she saw only his betrayal, replaying it over and over in her mind. Every word he spoke felt like a lie. Every kindness seemed suspicious.

She thought the anger was protecting her, but in truth, it was **consuming** her.

And then came the fruit.

Her words, once warm, turned sharp. She spoke, and the bitterness dripped into every conversation. Her laughter—once so easy, so full—was now rare, hollow. She couldn't let him in, couldn't let herself believe in him again, because to trust him meant risking pain.

And so she held on to the anger.

Daniel tried. He was patient. He apologized. He did everything she asked—until, eventually, he stopped trying as hard.

Not because he didn't love her. But because love cannot grow where it is not received.

The distance between them widened, and still, Elena told herself she was protecting herself. That she wasn't ready. That she couldn't let go of the pain, because if she did—what was left to hold onto?

And so, like the tree, she stood alone.

One autumn afternoon, a healer came to the village. She was old, with silver hair and steady hands, and she had seen trees like this before. She walked to the well, knelt beside it, and touched the stones.

"The water is poisoned," she said.

The villagers nodded. "We know. We stopped drinking from it long ago."

The healer shook her head. "That's not enough. The tree is still drinking."

They hesitated. "But the tree is already lost," one of them said.

The healer looked up at its branches, at the darkened bark and the untouched fruit. She placed her hand against it, closed her eyes.

"No," she said. "It is still alive. It only needs the source to be cleansed."

And so they began. They dug deep, pulling up the soil, searching for the place where the poison had seeped in. They cleared it away, let fresh water flow. It took time, but the change was certain. The tree did not heal overnight.

But season by season, the bark brightened. The leaves grew full again. And when the fruit finally came, the healer took one in her hands, broke it open, and smiled.

It was sweet.

Elena stood at the edge of her own poisoned well, staring at the reflection in its dark waters. She saw the lines of sorrow etched into her face, the weight of anger pressing down on her shoulders.

And for the first time, she asked herself, **What if I could be healed?**

For so long, she had believed that letting go of the anger meant letting Daniel off the hook. That if she released the pain, it would mean his betrayal didn't matter.

But the truth was, the anger had not protected her. It had poisoned her.

And if she did not release it, if she did not let God cleanse the source of her pain, she would never know love again—not with Daniel, not with anyone. Because she had already walled herself inside a prison of her own making.

So she knelt.

She did not yet know how to let go, but she knew she could not stay here, in this place, drinking from the same poisoned well.

She placed her hands on the ground, as if feeling for the roots of her own soul, and she whispered the words that terrified her.

"God, help me let go."

And deep within her, something shifted.

It would take time. Healing always does.

But one day, when her heart bore fruit again, it would no longer be poison. It would be life.

Field Notes:

1. Situation Report:

Where did this chapter hit home for me?

2. Operational Insight:

What truth or principle stands out to me the most?

3. Action Step:

What's one small thing I will do differently this week because of this chapter?

4. Words to Say:

Who needs to hear something from me?

5. Brief Prayer:

Write a one-sentence prayer asking God to strengthen your character in this area.

Feeding The Hungry Man

How do you Handle a Hungry Man?

In the late 60's, Cambells Soup came out with a line of *"rich and hearty soups"* marketed to housewives that were supposed to appeal to their husbands' appetites. Afterall, everyone knows that men have voracious appetites that must be fed, or they will fail to be real men. That Jingle, "how do you handle a hungry man…?" became an earworm and was the most successful part of that marketing effort. I don't think the same can be said about the soup itself.

Marketing to men's appetites has strong message potential. I still laugh when I see replays of a classic tv commercial from the early 2000's for **Hungry Man TV Dinners**. The one I recall is of two men on an emergency team during a rain terrible storm. They are hurriedly building a wall of sandbags to hold back a flood with a bunch of other men. Randomly, as they labor hard, one man turns to the man next to him, shouting over the sound of the wind and askes, "So whad'ya have for dinner?" obviously eluding to the fact that he was powering through the hard work with ease.

The other man shouts back, "A pound of fried chicken, mashed potatoes and gravy, corn and puddin, and you?"

The first man struggle to be heard over the wind, crying out, " A sliver of trout, spritzed with lemon, and baby carrots…ahhhhhhh." as he is suddenly is sucked away into the wind, implying that he is too light and weak to stay planted on the ground and continue in this hard and demanding work with the other men. The moral, "*Should have had a Hungry Man dinner from Swanson's.*"

We know men are *hungry*. But the type of hungriness that men have, the voraciousness that wants to be filled is not a hunger that can be satisfied with food. Yes, many men try to fill that hunger with food. I know because I have done so myself. Others try to fill it with love, companionship, family, sex, fortune, fame, power, position, possessions, anger, drugs, drink, dominance, conquest, women, the list can be endless. The hunger that burns in men is a product of the fallen nature of man, not the need for food, clothing, shelter, or even love.

This nature of fallenness is something all humans are subject to. So why do some men seem to be enslaved at a deeper level than others? Why are some men more prone to addiction or dysfunction more than others? Why do some men's lives get defined by the hunger where others seem to strive to survive despite the common denominator of our fallen nature. The answer is in our ability to apply the cure versus to indulge the dysfunction.

The dysfunction is the *sickness*. When you embrace the limitations and demands of the dysfunction, you enable it to define life and set the course for all other considerations. When I was in high school, like most young men, I was trying to determine what my interests were, and how that could define my career. I spent many hours in our schools career center, viewing film loops, reading info packets, and talking with the counselor about things of interest. I would then go home and talk to my dad about them. The one career that was top of my list was forestry. It checked all the boxes for me. And I was sure that was it. But, he talked me out of it multiple times until I simply gave up. He was so afraid of my limp lungs that he could not define my future with any hope. He said, "foresters must work hard, cut fire lines, hike long distances, and be in physically demanding circumstances. You can't do those things." So I gave up. Eventually, twenty years later, I finally found a career that I liked. But I wasted the in-between years doing things I hated. I became bounded by the illness of my childhood. From that lesson, I learned some things, things that I can now teach with insight to others. This is one of those things. Despite how you begin, from any brokenness, you can find healing.

So, do not define yourself by your dysfunction one moment longer. You must define yourself by the cure, and the cure is God's original plan for you. That plan is **_purpose._** He said that before He formed you in your mother's womb that He knew you! What a wonderfully awesome statement that is. This means that the God that created all things knew who you were, who you would become, and made you intentionally to be that person from the beginning. So, despite what you may think or feel in any given moment, you are not a mistake or an accident. You were and remain intentional. And if you are intended, then there is a reason. And that reason is purpose.

So what is the dysfunction and what is the cure? We can name the dysfunction, it is narcissism. No, not the grandiose, look at me I'm awesome sort of narcissism. And not necessarily the type of narcissism that rises to the level of a mental health disorder. Leave those definitions behind you for now. We are talking about a specific kind of narcissism that is both common and curable. This type of narcissism is called _Hungry Narcissism (N. Brown)_. There are other terms for it, but I like Dr Brown's term because it brings clear understanding to the symptoms. A hungry narcissist is just that, hungry. There is that voracious appetite that can't be satisfied. The hunger exists for a reason, a reason unique to the individual. That reason, whatever it is, gnaws at the soul, and gives rise to the insatiable hunger ever seeking to be fed. The narcissist lives to find a person or people or circumstances to supply feeding.

So, how do you feed a hungry man who has a hole in his bucket that prevents his ever being filled up? Simple. We fist figure out what caused the hole. Then we create a plug for that hole that actually fits, by meeting that very specific need with a specific answer. You see, the things that a hungry narcissist has used most of his life to fill the hole have never actually fit the hole, so the hole has never been sealed off. This is why he can never get satiated. He just demands more and more supply. But if he had the right fix, he could fill up and be restored. His bucket of purpose could once more be full, and he could resume his path to achieving intended outcomes.

I have included a short survey at the end of this chapter for you to take, and to have your closets family or friends to take with you, to help you determine if you are struggling with hungry narcissism. If you are, use the points of the survey to begin to seek the cause of you original hurt that made the hole. Seek out professional help if you need it, and ask God to search your heart and reveal what you need

Field Notes:

1. Situation Report:

Where did this chapter hit home for me?

2. Operational Insight:

What truth or principle stands out to me the most?

3. Action Step:

What's one small thing I will do differently this week because of this chapter?

4. Words to Say:

Who needs to hear something from me?

5. Brief Prayer:

Write a one-sentence prayer asking God to strengthen your character in this area.

Tomorrow For Sure!

Procrastination: The Never-Ending Cycle of Self-Defeat

I used to work for a lady who owned a lot of rental property. About half of her rental property were actually old single-wide trailers. Her husband had installed them some 10 to 20 years prior to the time I worked for her, when they were old but not ancient. These trailers were purchased used and placed on property before the local building codes prevented it. He was able to place quite a few on the property and he wired them up, brought water in from a central water system, and installed his own septic systems, kind of under the table so to speak. Most of them didn't have permits because they were out in a rural area that was unincorporated at the time, so was off the county's *development & planning* radar. Over the years they required *a lot* of maintenance to keep them viable.

When he passed away she hired me to, among other things, look after and manage these properties. As I got deeper into these properties I continue to find more and more amazing problems with them. There were a lot of funny stories behind them, some of them not funny in a laughable way but more funny in the "oh my god!" way. We had this inside slogan that spoke to our fears, the fear that some day one of these "wobble boxes" as old trailers are unaffectionately called, would go up in flames and hurt or even kill a tenant or their family. *"Frontier Rentals, Nobody's Died Yet!"* Understand, gallows humor is a way of dissipating fear and anxiety when one feels they can't control their circumstances. And there were times that being associated with this group of death traps kept me awake at night.

I was constantly running across strange adaptations of prior repairs that tended to make no sense. Some of them were downright dangerous. I hesitate to even tell you about them. One of the stories that I had heard about but didn't witness myself, of a sewage backup on a rural property. The maintenance person contacted the owner and told her there was a problem with a particular house's septic system. She had ordered a septic service to come out and pump the tank and repair or unclog the lines, normal procedure in these cases. About an hour later, she received a message from the technicians dispatcher who requested she come to the site and advise him on what she wanted to do, because there was a serious problem. So she drove out to see what all the fuss was. As a real Estate professional, she was very aware of how to deal with septic systems, and was frustrated that they were unable to do something this simple, and went in with her guns ready to dray. "What's the problem, just pump the septic tank!" she shouted at the driver, "Don't waste my time!"

According to the handyman who shared the story, the driver tried to keep a straight face, but returned, "I wish I could, ma'am, but you don't have a septic tank, you have a Chevy."

When she looked puzzled he carefully explained that it appeared that someone didn't actually install a septic tank, but instead had buried an old car, rolled up the windows, and ran a pipe into a hole in the roof, and then the effluent leached out of holes in the trunk into the septic field area. That was his makeshift septic system.

Well this was funny, it was also a disaster. Of course, she knew in an instant what had happened. Her late husband was notorious for doing such things. She called these his "*for-nows*." He would make a fast, supposedly temporary fix "for now" and then move on to something new, seldom if ever returning to make a permanent fix. He was famous for his "*for-nows*." Somewhere harmless. Some were disastrous. One of his *for-nows* was a quick wiring repair on the camper that they owned, which they drove up into the mountains, and which, along the way, subsequently shorted out and caught fire. She told me they barely got out of the thing in time before it was engulfed in flames, and quickly burnt down to the chassis.

Another for now that I witnessed, he had taken The wires from two 110 volt circuits and join them together in order to have a 220 volt portable heater in the dining room without considering that he was pulling that 220 volts from the same side of the electrical box rather than two separate sides, therefore drawing way too much current. One day when I came to the house to check on his wife I walked in the front door, she was in the back of the house, and there were flames coming out of the wall socket. He was clever, but not clever enough.

You see, his for-now's were a form of pathological procrastination. He did what he needed to do minimally to get to what he *wanted* to have done *in the moment* and figured he'd come back later and fix things, or make them permanent, but he was really too easily distracted to follow-up. So, as long as they were good enough *for now* he could wait.

Tomorrow was when he was going to get to it. But the entire property was littered with for-now's. He had half-finished projects everywhere. He had rooms that had been started and not finished. He had plumbing that was started and not finished. He had landscape that was started and not finished. He had a barn that was started and not finished. He had a herd of cattle he had started and not finished. He had a development he had started and not finished. He had so many things he had started in not finished. Everything was started, just enough to scratch the itch of ambition, then he went on to the next thing thinking I'll get to that later but it's good enough for now. This is a form of procrastination based on self-indulging a whim. It testifies to a lack of objective planning, a sense of purpose and design. It lacks specific forethought and strategic goals and methods to operational success. It violates principles and processes to create the illusion of success for now...

> *"Tomorrow is the day when idlers work, and fool reform, and mortal men lay hold on heaven."*
>
> – Edward Young (c. 3 July 1683 – 5 April 1765)[3]

Procrastination, often framed as harmless postponement, is more insidious than it appears. It is not simply a delay in action; it is a cycle of self-defeat. At its core lies a faulty paradigm: the belief that tomorrow will provide the ideal circumstances for productivity or change. However, the reality is that "tomorrow" is an illusion—a concept that perpetually moves forward, never allowing us to catch it. This truth is aptly summarized in the quote, "Tomorrow's the day that idle men work; tomorrow's the day that fools repent."

The Illusion of Tomorrow

The phrase "I'll do it tomorrow" offers temporary comfort, masking the anxiety or discomfort of taking action today. Yet, as each new day becomes "today," tomorrow remains

---

[3] The Complaint: or, Night-Thoughts on Life, Death, & Immortality, better known simply as Night-Thoughts, is a long poem by Edward Young published in nine parts (or "nights") between 1742 and 1745.

perpetually out of reach. This flawed reasoning convinces us that our good intentions are enough to justify our delay. But intentions without action are powerless, leading to an endless loop of postponement. By relying on the promise of a tomorrow that never arrives, procrastinators rob themselves of the opportunity to act in the only moment they truly have—now.

The illusion of tomorrow is further compounded by our tendency to overestimate our future capabilities while underestimating the effort required. We imagine that tomorrow we will be more motivated, better prepared, or less distracted. In reality, procrastination makes the task harder to approach over time. Anxiety, guilt, and unfinished obligations accumulate, creating a burden that makes starting even more difficult.

Self-Defeat Through Delay

Procrastination is self-defeating because it prioritizes immediate comfort over long-term fulfillment. While we may temporarily avoid stress by delaying action, the consequences inevitably catch up with us, often amplifying the very stress we sought to escape. Missed opportunities,

unfulfilled potential, and damaged trust in ourselves erode our confidence. The cycle of procrastination feeds on this erosion, creating a downward spiral of avoidance and regret.

The quote, "Tomorrow's the day that idle men work; tomorrow's the day that fools repent," underscores the futility of relying on tomorrow for what could—and should—be done today. Idle men postpone effort, trusting in a mythical future where work will somehow become easier or more appealing. Similarly, fools put off repentance, imagining a time when it will be more convenient to make amends or change their ways. Both groups share a common flaw: they waste the only resource that truly matters—time.

Breaking the Cycle

To escape the cycle of procrastination, we must challenge the faulty paradigm that tomorrow holds the key to our success. The first step is recognizing that "tomorrow" will never be more conducive to action than today. Life does not grant us perfect conditions; it requires us to act despite imperfection. Embracing this truth helps us focus on the present, where meaningful change is possible.

Accountability is another powerful tool in overcoming procrastination. By setting specific deadlines and breaking large tasks into smaller, manageable steps, we create a sense of urgency and accomplishment. Additionally, cultivating a mindset of discipline over motivation can help us act consistently, even when we don't feel like it. Motivation is fleeting, but

discipline ensures progress.

Finally, we must shift our perspective on failure. The fear of imperfection often paralyzes procrastinators, but failure is not the enemy—inaction is. Viewing mistakes as opportunities for growth rather than evidence of inadequacy empowers us to take risks and learn from them. The only true failure is the failure to try.

Procrastination is a deceptive habit rooted in the illusion of tomorrow. By deferring action to a day that never comes, we trap ourselves in a never-ending cycle of avoidance and regret. The wisdom of the quote, "Tomorrow's the day that idle men work; tomorrow's the day that fools repent," reminds us of the urgency of living

intentionally today. Breaking free from procrastination requires rejecting the myth of tomorrow, embracing the imperfect present, and taking deliberate steps toward our goals. In doing so, we reclaim our time, our purpose, and our potential.

Field Notes:

1. Situation Report:

Where did this chapter hit home for me?

2. Operational Insight:

What truth or principle stands out to me the most?

3. Action Step:

What's one small thing I will do differently this week because of this chapter?

4. Words to Say:

Who needs to hear something from me?

5. Brief Prayer:

Write a one-sentence prayer asking God to strengthen your character in this area.

Maybe it's time to Pop the Hood

Have you ever seen a man standing in front of his car with the hood popped open, gazing at the engine?

He's staring, clearly puzzled about what might be wrong, but he probably has no idea where to start. He hopes that by looking closely, he'll spot a loose wire, a broken hose, or some obvious issue. However, with modern cars' complexity, he often doesn't know what to look for. Eventually, he'll need to consult an expert for a diagnosis or, at the very least, have the diagnostic codes read. This is because he lacks a true understanding of how a modern car functions and doesn't possess the skills to decipher its issues. Unfortunately, no one has taught him, or he simply isn't equipped to do it.

In a similar way, to many men, women operate like a sophisticated, computerized automobile, serving as the central processing unit in the relationship. In contrast, men resemble older cars with simpler mechanical parts that can be adjusted with basic tools. Women are wired in a complex, interconnected manner that offers a level of synchronicity that often baffles men. To bridge the understanding gap between men and women, some diagnostic tools are necessary. When issues arise in a marriage, men frequently find themselves in stunned silence, standing with the hood open, looking at their wives, hoping that if they stare long enough, they might discover a solution. If he realizes he can't fix it himself, he might slam the hood shut, downplay the situation, and hope that the metaphorical "check engine" light will turn off on its own. In a moment of desperation, he might seek advice or agree to see a pastor or counselor to get those diagnostic codes checked.

This is the typical approach many men take toward maintaining their marriages. It's not that they don't care—they genuinely do. Rather, they often feel inadequate, under-skilled, or unqualified, and these feelings can be overwhelming. As a result, they tend to avoid confronting the problem, hoping that nothing serious will happen. This mindset can be seen in many men across various situations: *"If it ain't broke, don't fix it."*

What if you could be different? What if you could take an advanced course in computerized marriage diagnostics before any issues arise? Imagine having a code reader on hand at all times, ready to plug into your marriage and reveal any warning signs. What if you practiced preventive maintenance consistently, so that the warning lights rarely illuminated before you knew something required attention? What if?

Perhaps it's time to lift the hood and use that code reader in advance. Preventive maintenance is the key to achieving a smoothly functioning and reliable marriage. Does that sound appealing to you? If so, I recommend you start by enrolling in an advanced course in marriage diagnostics. A little insight: your wife may have already begun this process. There are several steps you can take to kick off your own diagnostics. Let's consider this from a man's perspective.

First, you could wait for the check engine light to illuminate.

In a marriage, what does the check engine light signify? When the light comes on in your car, it means something is wrong, but you may not immediately know what it is. Similarly, when the check engine light blinks in your marriage, one of two scenarios is occurring:

a) Your wife is confronting you about something she perceives as an issue, or there is a broader problem in the relationship. This is when the warning light first appears, and you're seeing it from an external perspective. Often, this manifests as, "Honey, we need to talk..." — phrases that can send a chill down any man's spine, tightening around his heart with anxiety.

b) You experience a surge of emotional panic, and suddenly the check engine light in your own mind is flashing, accompanied by alarm bells signaling that something is amiss—like the klaxon alarm on the bridge of the Enterprise when Captain Kirk sounds a red alert.

In either case, the check engine light is shining bright red, indicating something is seriously wrong. Everything must pause, and we need to shift into triage mode. It's essential to determine what the issue is and decide whether to halt, repair, or escape from it.

When someone confronts you and tells you that something is wrong—whether with you or your circumstances—it typically feels like uninvited and unpleasant feedback. Most people do not appreciate being confronted in this way. Defenses rise immediately, or an escape route is sought. Men instinctively respond with a fight-or-flight reaction, either fleeing from danger or, if flight is not an option, resorting to fighting. This response is natural and occurs almost instantaneously due to the adrenaline surge during stressful situations, making it hard to control. However, since many of our perceived threats originate within our personal lives—often stemming from the well-meaning intentions of our wives—our fight-or-flight responses are often directed at them, even though this is not our intention. Sometimes this frustration extends to the children or even manifests in misplaced anger towards a pet. This behavior relates to the old adage about "killing the messenger." It's akin to being angry with your car when it breaks down: it's usually not the car's fault; more often, it's a result of your own neglect in maintenance. Nevertheless, when the car fails, frustration is directed at it.

Similarly, when a marriage falters, it may be due to a lack of maintenance, yet often the blame falls on the relationship itself. The better approach would be to prioritize preventative maintenance. But what does that entail? The answer, while daunting for many men, can lead to greater long-term happiness: simply ask your partner how she feels about the marriage. Inquire about her well-being and whether there are areas where you could improve. I understand that this can be intimidating, as she may respond by expressing that things aren't going well. Men tend to neglect fixing problems they aren't aware of, but this attitude ignores the importance of preventive maintenance. Just because you don't see water leaking in your crawl space, termites damaging your home, or dry rot in your rafters doesn't mean that these issues don't exist. What remains unseen can indeed cause harm.

So, ask. Not only will this help you uncover any building problems, but it will also strengthen your emotional connection with your wife, demonstrating your commitment to the relationship. By engaging in these conversations, you can begin to address any damage or potential issues before they escalate. This approach yields a win-win-win situation: she benefits from a deeper connection, the relationship improves as you address concerns proactively, and you avoid future complications that could undermine your happiness.

Below is an example of a monthly diagnostic survey you can use to assess your performance. This survey can serve as a conversation starter with your wife, or you can hand it to her and say, "Hey babe, I know I'm awesome, but I want to know how awesome." On a scale of 1 to 10, ask her to rate you on various aspects. Then, step back and hope for a good score. There's also a version for your children; ask them how you're doing as a dad. Of course, you probably won't receive all tens unless it's allowance day, but this will provide a snapshot of how your family feels about your efforts. If you take their feedback seriously, it can help you become a better person. This is just one approach.

I've also included a tool I developed called the Love in Me tool. This tool is based on 1 Corinthians 13, which describes love in the agape sense—unconditional love that remains steadfast regardless of the other person's actions. It represents a commitment: "I will love you this way, no matter what." The tool includes a list of love's attributes and a list of behaviors that love will not engage in. When applied correctly, it demonstrates how love manifests and prevails. 1 Corinthians 13 is more than just a poem; it's a model for love. Using the Love in Me tool allows you to evaluate the quality of your love—an essential diagnostic for your marriage—on a weekly basis. You can rate yourself, receive feedback from your spouse, and conduct proactive maintenance.

Utilizing one or both of these tools can significantly help you. Checking in weekly is a practical way to ensure your marriage is thriving. Remember, asking for input before it's offered can make the process easier. When someone feels compelled to give feedback, it often indicates a problem you might be ignoring. By the time they dare to share their thoughts, it's usually because you've caused them frustration or pain. If you ask for their opinions early on, you are likely to be more open to receiving it, resulting in less hurt feelings and encouraging more honest feedback.

This increases the chances of achieving a win-win situation. Waiting for a 'check engine' light usually leads to conflict, which, while not inherently bad, can be uncomfortable to navigate. This form is to help you have meaningful dialog about key issues.

SPOUSE SURVEY

This is FEEDBACK not criticism. Please build your partner up, not tear down, while being honest.

Dear wife, please rate my efforts as you see them on a scale of 1–10.

1= Very Negative	6= A Bit Positive
2 = A Little Negative	7= More Positive
3= Negative	8= Positive
4= No Affect	9 = Very Positive
5 = Hardley Better	10 = A Big Difference

___ How do you feel about my level of action and responsibility in our partnership?

___ How has my overall mood seemed to you?

___ How loved have you felt lately?

___ Have I contributed to you feeling emotionally satisfied lately?

___ How do you feel about my efforts to maintain my physical health?

___ How satisfied are you with our sexual intimacy?

___ How are you feeling about our financially security?

___ How safe do you feel with me in public?

___ How do you feel about my interactions with our children?

___ How do you feel about my partnership with you as a parent?

___ How well have I led the family spiritually in the past month?

___ How have I spoken your primary love language this month? (gifts, time, service, touch, words)

1. What's one thing you wish I would start doing or do more of?

_____
_____

2. What's one thing you wish I would stop doing or do less of?

_____
_____

What else do you need to say?

_____
_____
_____
_____

The LOVnME Tool
2024 © all rights reserved

The Commitment: *We will set aside* each _____(day) at ___o'clock to focus on improving the expression of LOVE in our marriage. We will pray that the Holy Spirit leads us to be standard bearers of God's images as Love in ***1 Corinthians 13***. *Celebrate!* (What went *very well* this last week?) e.g., Patience • Kindness • Other

_____

Our Desired Outcomes

Beginning with the end in mind, select up to three Loving Outcomes from the list below. These will be your ***outcome goals*** of the week.

For Her	For Him
Love ***rejoices*** *with* the truth.	Love ***rejoices*** *with* the truth.
It always ***protects***,	It always ***protects***,
It always ***trusts***,	It always ***trusts***,
It always ***hopes***,	It always ***hopes***,
It always ***perseveres***.	It always ***perseveres***.
Love never fails.	Love never fails.

Set the Standards

Pick a combination of constructive *attributes, or destructive* attributes you wish to work on this week to support your outcome goal(s). (limit to 3 total).

For Her	For Him

Love IS…	Love IS…
Love is patient,	Love is patient,
Love is kind.	Love is kind.
Love is NOT…	Love is NOT…
Does not envy,	Does not envy,
Does not boast,	Does not boast,
Is not proud.	Is not proud.
Is not rude,	Is not rude,
Is not self-seeking,	Is not self-seeking,
Is not easily angered,	Is not easily angered,
Keeps no record of wrongs.	Keeps no record of wrongs.

Taking Action

Dedicate yourselves to working on these standards by choosing actions that are standards or goal-driven for the next week.

Join together *next week at the pre-agreed day and time* to review how you each view the results.

Evaluate your actions and honestly rate how you feel *YOU* did on your goals between 1 & 10, 1 meaning that "I did not make any changes", and 10 meaning "I strongly accomplished my goal(s),". Then, ask for feedback.

My Opinion of My Progress This Week	
For Her	For Him
Love *rejoices with* the truth.	Love *rejoices with* the truth.
It always *protects*,	It always *protects*,
It always *trusts*,	It always *trusts*,
It always *hopes,*	It always *hopes,*
It always perseveres.	It always perseveres.
Love never fails.	Love never fails.

My Spouse's Rating of My Progress This Week	
For Her	For Him
Love *does not* delight in evil but *rejoices with* the truth.	Love *does not* delight in evil but *rejoices with* the truth.
It always *protects*,	It always *protects*,
It always *trusts*,	It always *trusts*,
It always *hopes,*	It always *hopes,*

| It always perseveres. | It always perseveres. | |
| Love never fails. | Love never fails. | **What** |

needs more work?
Constructive Feedback for Him:
_____
_____

Constructive Feedback for Her:
_____
_____

Once you feel you have heard and been heard from all sides, set your outcome goals for next week. If appropriate, continue the ones from this last week that need more practice.

Field Notes:

1. Situation Report:
Where did this chapter hit home for me?

2. Operational Insight:
What truth or principle stands out to me the most?

3. Action Step:
What's one small thing I will do differently this week because of this chapter?

4. Words to Say:
Who needs to hear something from me?

5. Brief Prayer:
Write a one-sentence prayer asking God to strengthen your character in this area.

The Truth Shall Set You Free

"Then you will know the truth, and the truth will set you free." — John 8:32

I. Breaking the Chains of "My Truth"

I was standing in the checkout line at a grocery store, behind a young man who looked like he was barely out of high school. Baggy hoodie, AirPods in, cart full of energy drinks and frozen pizzas. He was arguing with the cashier about something — a store policy, I think. His voice was rising, and the words that cut through the buzz of the store were sharp and defensive.

"Well, that's just my truth," he said, raising his eyebrows as if that settled the matter.

The cashier, an older woman with the patience of a saint, blinked and simply nodded.

The phrase stuck with me.

"My truth."

We hear it everywhere now. On talk shows. In interviews. From influencers and college students and even pastors. It's the cultural safe word for "you're not allowed to disagree with me."

But deep down, that phrase reveals something much more troubling: we've replaced *truth* with *perspective*, and assumed they're the same.

They're not.

Consider a man named Alan who worked in construction. Good guy, hard worker, but cynical to the core. He used to say, "Everyone's out for themselves, man. No one cares. You can only count on yourself." That was his mantra. And it seemed believable — until the day he collapsed from heat exhaustion on a rooftop in the middle of July.

Without hesitation, the rest of the crew ran to his aid. Two men carried him down a ladder. One ran to get cold towels. Another called 911.

Alan came to with water in his hand and three guys hovering over him. He blinked in disbelief. "Why'd you all do that?"

He wasn't being sarcastic. He was genuinely confused.

That moment — that disconnect between his belief and his experience — stuck with him. A few months later, he asked someone on the crew, "Do you think it's possible I've been wrong about people?"

Alan wasn't lying when he said, "you can only count on yourself." He believed it. But belief doesn't make it true.

Men, let's be honest: we all carry stories that shape how we see the world. But not every story tells the truth.

Some stories keep us locked in bitterness. Others keep us trapped in pride. Still others quietly whisper lies about God, about others, and about ourselves.

That's why truth — real truth — matters. Because only *the* truth has the power to break the chains of our *version* of it.

II. What Is Truth?

In 2017, a men's retreat was held on a working ranch in Wyoming. Between sessions, a group of guys were throwing hatchets at a tree stump target — part stress relief, part primitive bonding. That's where Carl opened up.

Carl was a truck driver with a strong handshake and a soft-spoken grief behind his eyes. Over burgers and coffee, he said, "I don't know what's true anymore. My wife said I was emotionally unavailable. My buddies said I dodged a bullet. My counselor says I need boundaries. Who do I believe?"

That night, sitting by a fire, a fellow attendee gently asked, "What do you believe about God?"

Carl shrugged. "I think He's real, but I don't know if He cares."

The man opened his Bible to John 14:6, where Jesus says: *"I am the way, the truth, and the life. No one comes to the Father except through me."*

They talked for an hour. Not about religion, but about Jesus — the man who didn't just speak truth but *embodied* it. Carl listened. Not politely — hungrily.

When truth is a person, not just a principle, you don't need to chase every opinion. You just follow Him.

Carl didn't become a theologian overnight, but he started reading the Gospel of John every morning in his cab. Months later, he said, "Turns out, truth wasn't as complicated as I made it. I just hadn't looked in the right place."

Truth isn't fragile. It doesn't fear examination. It just waits — patiently — to be found.

III. The Emotional Lens of "My Truth"

There's a man named Darren — a high school football coach, known for his discipline and booming voice. But behind the scenes, Darren was terrified of vulnerability.

When he was eleven, his father disappeared. One day they were fishing; the next, gone without explanation. His mother shut down emotionally. Darren learned early:

"Don't count on anyone. Don't feel. Don't show weakness."

Fast forward twenty-five years: Darren's marriage was cracking. His wife said she felt like she was married to a stranger. "I'm doing everything right," he said. "But it's never enough."

A counselor asked him, "What would it mean to let her in?"

He looked panicked. "I can't. I don't trust people with my insides."

That was Darren's truth — but not *the* truth.

Through counseling, Scripture, and painfully honest prayer, Darren started confronting the narrative he'd been carrying. He began to recognize that his emotional isolation wasn't strength — it was self-protection.

Healing didn't come overnight. But as Darren dismantled his emotional defenses, he began to experience something new: connection. Wholeness. Peace.

When we confuse emotional experience with eternal truth, we limit what God can do. Our lens becomes our Lord. But truth — real, eternal truth — gently dismantles our defenses and heals what's underneath.

IV. The Nature of Absolute Truth

At a campus Bible study, a college student named Luke raised a common objection. "I don't think any one religion can claim to have all the truth. Isn't that arrogant?"

Another student drew a dot on a whiteboard. "Let's say this represents *all* the knowledge in the universe — everything that's true. How much do you think you personally understand?"

Luke smirked. "A grain of sand's worth, maybe."

"Exactly. So if God is real, wouldn't He need to *reveal* truth to us — not just leave us to figure it out?"

The room fell quiet.

Absolute truth doesn't mean we know everything absolutely. It means there *is* something solid — something outside us — that can be trusted regardless of our feelings.

God hasn't left us in the dark. He gave us Scripture — not as a textbook, but as a lamp (Psalm 119:105). He sent Jesus — not just to teach, but to *be* the truth.

If truth were a mountain, we wouldn't climb our way up with intellect and morality. We'd need it to descend to us.

And it did. In Bethlehem. In flesh. In grace and truth.

V. Truth and Freedom: A Man's Path to Integrity

There was a pastor — Nathan — who preached every Sunday, counseled families, and was slowly unraveling from a hidden addiction to prescription painkillers.

"I feel like a fraud," he confessed. "But if I come clean, I'll lose everything."

A friend replied, "You've already lost the most important thing — your freedom."

Nathan broke. Tears. Silence. Surrender.

He confessed to his elders, took time off, entered recovery. When he returned to the pulpit a year later, he said, "I used to think truth was something I preached. Now I know it's something I live."

Truth isn't just known — it's walked. Practiced. And costly. But it leads to integrity.

And integrity — being the same man in private as you are in public — is the call on every Christian man's life.

VI. The Role of Discipline in Truth

Greg was an IT manager, father of three, volunteer at church — and exhausted from wearing masks. With his boss, he was assertive. With his friends, sarcastic. At home, withdrawn.

It wasn't until his son asked, "Dad, why do you smile more at your phone than at us?" that it hit him.

Greg began getting up earlier. Reading the Bible. Asking two men from church to hold him accountable. He told his wife, "I'm tired of being fragments. I want to be whole."

Over time, he became a man anchored in truth — not by perfection, but by daily practice.

Discipline isn't legalism. It's spiritual fitness. And like muscle, truth is built with reps.

VII. The Truth in Relationships

Sam and Drew had been best friends since college. But when Drew began drinking more and withdrawing, Sam stayed silent.

Until one night, Drew stumbled into his son's baseball game reeking of alcohol. Sam drove him home and said nothing.

The next day, Sam's wife said, "You're not helping him by staying quiet."

That afternoon, Sam sat on Drew's porch and said, "I love you, and I can't keep pretending everything's fine."

Drew didn't fight, he wept.

That conversation marked the start of healing. Truth spoken in love had cut through shame.

Truth in relationships requires courage. But silence is not kindness.

VIII. Standing Firm in a Shifting World

Ben, a public high school teacher, was asked to remove biblical references from his curriculum — even literary ones.

He refused. Quietly. Respectfully. Clearly.

He lost his position. Got reassigned. Fewer students. Less influence. But more peace.

His former students still sought him out: "You were the only adult who didn't flinch."

Truth has a cost in a culture of compromise. But the cost of abandoning it is far greater: the erosion of courage.

IX. Final Words: Live Free, Lead Well

Across the country, in Kentucky, a group of men meet at 6 a.m. every Saturday. They open Scripture, drink burnt coffee, and ask the hard questions.

"What lie are you believing this week?"

"Where are you pretending?"

"Who are you afraid to tell the truth to?"

One man — Terrence — once said, "I spent 20 years building a version of myself that looked good but couldn't weather a storm. Truth stripped all that down. Now I'm free."

That's the goal.

Not perfection. Freedom.

Not swagger. Substance.

Not your truth. *The* Truth.

Jesus Christ — who is the Truth — invites you into the light. Into freedom. Into wholeness.

Walk in it.

Key Scriptures for Reflection:

John 8:32 — "Then you will know the truth, and the truth will set you free."

John 14:6 — "I am the way and the truth and the life."

Psalm 119:105 — "Your word is a lamp for my feet, a light on my path."

Proverbs 18:17 — "The first to plead his case seems right, until another comes and examines him."

Romans 12:2 — "Do not conform to the pattern of this world..."

Field Notes:

1. Situation Report:

Where did this chapter hit home for me?

2. Operational Insight:

What truth or principle stands out to me the most?

3. Action Step:

What's one small thing I will do differently this week because of this chapter?

4. Words to Say:

Who needs to hear something from me?

5. Brief Prayer:

Write a one-sentence prayer asking God to strengthen your character in this area.

Thinking Outside What Box?

We've all heard it said before. You need to think outside the box. The problem is we don't know what the box is. We don't know what's inside the box. How in the world are we going to know what's outside the box? The box is the boundaries that surround us and tell us how things are done. We might call the box common sense. We might call the box how things are done. We might call the box the right thing to do. The problem with thinking outside the box is that the box tells us right from wrong in a lot of context. If we know that we're supposed to drive on the right hand side of the road, and something suddenly happens in front of us that is dangerous we are going to swerve to the right. Because that's what the box tells us. But as most of us know when there is an emergency sometimes swerving to the left makes more sense. That is outside the box. But our instinct is

the swerve to the right. In a flash of insight though we might swerve to the left. This is how people end up in the median. But sometimes serving to the left is also dangerous. And somehow some, some way, we have to figure out which way to go to create the best outcome.

I read a book once years ago, a book and an author whose names I can't remember, the talked about people who are natural survivors. People who tend to be aware naturally. When they get on a plane they know where the exits are. They know who's around them. They know what the dangers are. When they're in public they're aware of who's around them. They know what the activities are. They have a sense. Other people go through life oblivious of the dangers and of the opportunities. In the book talked about not only the natural

tendency to be aware, but of the ability to build the skill of awareness. Such as, learning when you go into a venue to pick a seat where you have a commanding view of the room so you can see danger enter the room or come toward you. It makes no sense for the husband or the father to sit with his back to the room. You cannot see danger coming and protect your children. Or your wife.

Thinking outside the box requires us to think about things through the lens of strengths weaknesses opportunities and threats. Better also asks us to think about more than that.

Thinking Outside the Box for Personal Life Development

Thinking outside the box means breaking free from conventional patterns and

embracing innovative strategies for personal growth. For men seeking to develop themselves, this approach requires intentional effort, a willingness to challenge preconceived notions, and the courage to explore new ideas. Here's how to cultivate this mindset and apply it to your life.

1. Redefine Success

Begin by questioning your definition of success. Many men equate success with external markers like wealth, status, or possessions. While these can be components of a fulfilling life, personal development is much deeper. True success involves growth in character, relationships, emotional intelligence, and a sense of purpose. Reflect on what truly matters to you—your core values—and use them as a compass to guide your decisions.

2. Challenge Old Habits

Habits are powerful but can become barriers when they keep you stuck in routine thinking. Identify habits that no longer serve your goals. For example, if your evenings are spent passively watching TV, consider using that time to read, exercise, or pursue a new hobby. Small changes to daily routines can create ripple effects that lead to broader transformation.

3. Seek Diverse Perspectives

One of the most effective ways to think outside the box is to expose yourself to diverse ideas and people. Engage with individuals who have different experiences, beliefs, or expertise. Listen to their stories, read books outside your usual genres, or attend events that challenge your worldview. Expanding your mental horizons sparks creativity and helps you approach your own challenges in fresh ways.

4. Use Creative Problem-Solving Techniques

Creative problem-solving isn't just for work; it's equally valuable in personal life. Techniques like brainstorming, mind mapping, or reverse thinking can help you approach goals differently. For example, instead of asking, "How can I get a promotion?" ask, "What skills or passions do I have that I'm not using?" This shift in perspective often reveals untapped opportunities.

5. Embrace Failure as Growth

Fear of failure keeps many men from stepping out of their comfort zones. Instead of avoiding risk, reframe failure as a learning experience. When you take calculated risks, you gain insights that help you grow. Ask yourself: "What can I learn from this situation?" or "How will this make me stronger?" This mindset fosters resilience and adaptability, both essential for personal development.

6. Develop a Strategic Vision

Thinking outside the box doesn't mean abandoning structure—it means applying innovative strategies within a clear framework. Create a vision for your life

that includes specific, measurable goals. For instance, if you want to improve your health, don't just aim to "get fit." Instead, develop a detailed plan with milestones, such as running a 5K, learning meal prep, or adopting mindfulness practices to reduce stress.

7. Experiment with New Roles

Challenge your identity by trying out new roles. Volunteer for leadership positions in your community, take up mentoring, or learn a skill unrelated to your career. These experiences can reveal hidden strengths and inspire you to think beyond the roles you currently occupy.

8. Regularly Reflect and Reassess

Schedule time for regular reflection. Journaling, prayer, or quiet meditation can help you evaluate your progress and refine your strategies. Ask yourself questions like, "Am I focusing on what truly matters?" or "What's holding me back from pursuing my best life?" Honest self-assessment ensures you stay aligned with your goals.

Conclusion

Thinking outside the box for personal development is not about discarding structure but about innovating within it. By redefining success, challenging habits, seeking diverse perspectives, and embracing growth through failure, you can develop creative strategies that lead to a more fulfilling and purpose-driven life. The journey may not always be easy, but it will be rewarding as you discover your unique potential and become the man you were meant to be.

Field Notes:

1. Situation Report:

Where did this chapter hit home for me?

2. Operational Insight:

What truth or principle stands out to me the most?

3. Action Step:

What's one small thing I will do differently this week because of this chapter?

4. Words to Say:

Who needs to hear something from me?

5. Brief Prayer:

Write a one-sentence prayer asking God to strengthen your character in this area.

Trigger Points

John was frustrated. His wife was constantly upset with him. It seemed that he could do nothing right in her eyes, no matter how hard he tried. Little things resulted in big arguments. Those arguments could last hours into the night, depriving both of sleep, and then linger into the next day or two as residual moodiness and avoidance. John finally came to counseling and asked for help. He wanted to know how to fix himself.

With some exploration of marital conflicts, counselors routinely uncover emotional triggers for the conflict, and unsurprisingly, these conflicts seldom turn out to be so much about the surface conflict as about the underlying triggers that exist in the partners. An emotional trigger can significantly impact a person, and cause extreme relational disruption over seemingly insignificant events. Because couples are often unaware of the connection between triggers and conflicts, arguments can become heated and cyclic, leaving the couple damaged and confused. Most people are ignorant of their own triggers, at least to the depth of those triggers, and certainly cannot comprehend the depth of triggers for others.

Triggers don't have to make sense to be significant or dramatic. For instance, someone who faints at the sight of blood (Vasovagal syncope) does so not because blood itself is harmful, but because their nervous system perceives the stimulus as overwhelming, activating an automatic response. Similarly, emotional triggers are deeply rooted in the individual's *internal experiences*, shaped by personal history, unresolved pain, or deeply ingrained fears. The person or situation that *activates* the trigger serves as a catalyst, *not the cause*. This distinction is vital for understanding that triggers are resident within the person experiencing them, arising from their unique internal landscape, rather than being the responsibility of the external person or event.

By recognizing this, individuals can focus on addressing their emotional responses and learning healthy coping mechanisms, fostering more compassionate and constructive relationships while reducing unnecessary blame. Likewise, spouses can learn to appreciate the traumatic content that undergirds the trigger, and take reasonable steps to help mitigate activating the trigger. While no outside person can prevent trigger activation, care and support can provide safety while the triggered person learns to navigate newer coping strategies.

Unraveling Emotional Triggers: Understanding and Managing Conflicts in Marriage

Emotional triggers in marriage often lurk beneath the surface of routine arguments and cyclic disputes, creating conflicts that may seem disproportionate to their apparent causes. These triggers are deeply ingrained responses that spouses may not even recognize, yet they powerfully influence reactions and interactions. Understanding and managing these triggers is not only essential for resolving current conflicts but also for nurturing long-term emotional intimacy and stability in a marriage.

Emotional triggers are specific reminders, situations, or behaviors that provoke an intense emotional reaction, often because they are linked to past trauma, unresolved conflicts, or significant stressors. By identifying and understanding these triggers, couples can start to disentangle the emotional responses from the topics of their arguments, allowing for more effective communication and problem-solving.

This following essay explores the dynamics of emotional triggers in marriage, illustrating how they can fuel recurring conflicts and providing strategies for couples to identify, manage, and ultimately neutralize these triggers.

Understanding Emotional Triggers in Marriage

Emotional triggers in marital relationships can vary widely but typically involve situations that evoke feelings of insecurity, abandonment, inadequacy, or powerlessness. These triggers might stem from childhood experiences, previous relationships, or even stresses unrelated to the marriage, like job pressure or social anxieties.

For example, if one spouse grew up in a household where financial instability was a constant source of tension, discussions about money in their current relationship might trigger an outsized emotional response. The actual conversation about household budgeting isn't just a practical discussion—it's laden with deeper fears and anxieties about security and stability.

The impact of these triggers on a marriage can be profound. They often lead to miscommunications and misinterpretations, as one spouse reacts not just to what is being said in the moment, but to a whole history of associated emotions and experiences. This can make conflicts escalate quickly and unexpectedly, as the emotional stakes are much higher than the logical context would suggest.

Identifying Common Emotional Triggers in Routine Arguments

To understand how routine arguments can escalate into significant conflicts, it's crucial to recognize the patterns that indicate the presence of emotional triggers. Often, these arguments are not about the topic at hand but are a surface expression of underlying emotional turmoil. For instance, a simple disagreement over who should do the dishes can explode into a heated argument about respect and appreciation.

Cyclic arguments are particularly indicative of deeper issues. These are disputes that reoccur frequently, each time more intense and unresolved. They often follow a predictable pattern where the initial topic of the argument quickly gets lost in the emotional reactions it triggers.

Consider a couple where one partner feels the other is not attentive enough. The trigger might not be the specific instances of inattentiveness but rather an underlying fear of being unloved or neglected, possibly stemming from earlier life experiences. Each occurrence doesn't just bring up that instance but all past instances, both within and outside of the current relationship.

Strategies for Managing Emotional Triggers

The first step in managing emotional triggers is for individuals to develop self-awareness about their own triggers. Practices like mindfulness, where one observes their thoughts and feelings without judgment, and journaling, where one records events and their emotional responses to them, can be incredibly helpful. These practices help individuals recognize the patterns in their emotional responses and begin to separate these from the immediate causes.

Communication techniques also play a crucial role. Techniques such as using 'I' statements allow individuals to express their feelings without blaming the other person, which can help keep discussions from becoming defensive or confrontational. For example, saying "I feel neglected when you don't call me during the day" instead of "You never call me; you don't care about me" can lead to a more constructive conversation.

Empathy is another critical element in dealing with emotional triggers. It involves trying to understand the emotional experiences of the other person, not just intellectually but also emotionally. When both partners in a marriage can empathize with each other's triggers, it becomes much easier to respond in ways that are soothing rather than aggravating.

Therapeutic Approaches to Resolving Trigger-Induced Conflicts

Professional help, such as couples therapy, can be pivotal in resolving emotional trigger-induced conflicts. Therapists can assist couples in identifying and understanding each partner's triggers, fostering a deeper mutual understanding and developing more effective communication strategies. Therapists use various methods, including cognitive-behavioral therapy (CBT) and emotionally focused therapy (EFT), to help couples break the cycle of reactivity and learn how to respond to each other in healthier ways.

One effective therapeutic approach is conflict resolution training. Couples can learn specific skills to defuse emotionally charged situations, such as taking timeouts to cool down, rephrasing to avoid misunderstandings, and establishing common ground rules for disagreements. These skills can prevent triggers from escalating into full-blown disputes.

Preventative measures are also crucial in managing emotional triggers. Regular emotional check-ins, where couples dedicate time to discuss ongoing issues and emotional states, can help prevent the buildup of resentment and misunderstanding. Relationship audits, similar to performance reviews in professional settings, can help couples assess their relationship's health and proactively address potential trigger points.

Emotional triggers play a significant role in marital conflicts, often fueling disproportionate reactions to routine disagreements. By understanding what triggers these emotional responses, couples can begin to communicate more effectively, avoiding unnecessary escalation. Strategies such as self-awareness, empathetic communication, and professional therapy are essential in managing these triggers.

This essay has explored the dynamics of emotional triggers and offered practical advice for couples facing such challenges. Embracing these strategies can transform potential conflicts into opportunities for growth and deeper understanding, ultimately enhancing marital stability and happiness.

By actively addressing and managing emotional triggers, couples can create a more supportive and understanding relationship environment, where both partners feel heard, valued, and loved. The journey of unraveling and neutralizing emotional triggers is not only about preventing conflicts but also about building a stronger, more resilient bond that can withstand the challenges of life together.

Field Notes:

1. Situation Report:
Where did this chapter hit home for me?

2. Operational Insight:
What truth or principle stands out to me the most?

3. Action Step:
What's one small thing I will do differently this week because of this chapter?

4. Words to Say:
Who needs to hear something from me?

5. Brief Prayer:
Write a one-sentence prayer asking God to strengthen your character in this area.

Less is More & When to Not To...
The Art of Not Solving Every Problem

"Carry each other's burdens, and in this way you will fulfill the law of Christ." — Galatians 6:2

"Each one should carry their own load." — Galatians 6:5

There's a paradox in those two verses, isn't there?

We're called to carry each other's burdens — that's brotherhood, compassion, empathy. But we're also called to carry our own loads — that's responsibility, boundaries, stewardship. As Christian men, we walk that tension daily. Especially with our wives, our children, our friends, and our communities.

One of the most useful tools I've ever learned — both as a counselor and as a man — is a concept rooted in the work of Alfred Adler and developed into practical application for parenting by Don Dinkmeyer and Gary D. McKay[4] . In particular, their work on understanding *who owns the problem"* has been a game-changer — not just for parenting, but for every relationship. It helps us distinguish when a problem is ours to solve, when we are simply called to be present, and when our intervention is more about control than care.

Let's take Jake for example. He had just settled into his recliner with a cold drink when his wife, Rachel, came into the living room and dropped onto the couch with a frustrated sigh.

"You will *not* believe what happened with Jenna again," she said.

Jake muted the game and turned toward her, giving her his full attention — well, sort of. His body faced her, but his mind was already scanning through what advice he'd

---

[4] *Dinkmeyer, D., & McKay, G. (1983). Systematic training for effective parenting of teens. American Guidance Service*

given her the *last* time Jenna caused drama. He was ready for this.

"She called me *again* to ask for help planning her anniversary party," Rachel continued. "But then she shot down every single idea I gave her, like she'd already decided what she wanted but just needed someone to make her feel important. I don't even know why I bother. I'm tired of always being the one who shows up for her."

Jake, feeling the rising tension in her voice, jumped in.

"Okay, well, sounds like she's using you. You just need to stop answering her calls for a while. Maybe take a break from the friendship. That'll send a message."

Rachel blinked. "What?"

"I mean," Jake said, "you've got a lot going on. She clearly doesn't respect your time. You shouldn't let her walk all over you like that."

Rachel stared at him for a moment. Her shoulders dropped — not in relief, but in resignation.

"I wasn't asking you to solve it," she said, voice flat. "I just needed to talk about it."

Jake, now suddenly aware he'd hit the wrong button, scrambled. "I just thought maybe—"

"I know what you were doing," she said. "I don't need a game plan, Jake. I needed someone to just *listen*."

She stood up and walked into the kitchen, leaving Jake sitting there, half-ashamed, half-defensive — and very much alone in his perfectly logical, unhelpful solution.

A few minutes later, still holding his drink, he thought back to that scene in *Cars* when Mater — after launching himself backward into a situation he wasn't supposed to be in — is reminded of what he was told.

"Mater, What did I tell you about doing that?" Mater, with that sheepish grin: *"To not to."*

Jake chuckled to himself and muttered under his breath, "Yeah… to not to."

Guys, sometimes the wisest thing we can do — especially when our wives are venting — is remember Mater's sage (if accidental) wisdom: **"To not to."**

Not every comment needs a comeback. Not every vent needs a verdict. Not every wound needs a workaround. Sometimes, your wife just needs you to *listen*, nod, say, "That sounds exhausting," and sit in it with her. That moment of empathy may be more healing than any five-point solution you could offer.

So next time you're tempted to fix it mid-sentence, just pause and ask yourself:

"Is this a time to help… or a time *to not to?*"

Because being a good man doesn't always mean being a problem-solver.

Sometimes, it just means being present.

Why Men Go Into Fix-It Mode

Let's start with a confession: I *love* fixing problems.

Give me a broken hinge, a leaking faucet, a complicated spreadsheet — I'm all in. There's something deeply satisfying about seeing an issue, identifying the solution, and knocking it out. Boom. Problem solved. Move on. If you're anything like me, you know exactly what I mean. Most men do.

We're wired this way. God made us to *build*, to *cultivate*, to *protect*. In Genesis 2, before sin entered the world, man was placed in the garden *to work it and to take care of it*. That desire to manage, organize, repair, and lead well? That's not toxic masculinity — that's godly design. But here's where it gets tricky. That same instinct that serves us so well in the garage or the boardroom can cause real problems in our relationships — especially with our wives, our kids, and our close friends. You see, not every problem needs solving. At least not by you. And not every moment calls for action.

As men, we sometimes misread the room. We hear frustration in someone's voice — and we interpret that as a job assignment. Our wives share something painful, and before they've even finished the sentence, we're mentally drafting a plan, writing out the steps, and explaining how they can "fix it" by tomorrow morning.

You know what usually follows? Silence. Sometimes confusion. Sometimes tears. Why? Because in our rush to solve the problem, we often miss the point. What they needed wasn't a fix — they needed *connection*. They needed to be heard, not managed. Understood, not diagnosed.

I remember a guy in one of my men's groups — we'll call him Todd — who said something that stuck with all of us. He said, "My wife told me, 'Every time I tell you something hard, I feel like you put on your hard hat and grab your toolbox. But sometimes, I just need you to sit on the porch with me.'" **That image hit home.**

Men, we have to learn to recognize that sometimes love looks like stillness, not solutions. It's not about suppressing your wiring — it's about maturing it. It's about learning when action is needed… and when your job is simply to be present, to be steady, to be safe. That's where emotional maturity comes in. That's where godly wisdom starts to shape our instincts. And that's where we turn to a powerful concept that's helped thousands of men, including me: Who owns the problem?

Who Owns the Problem?

The first time I came across this idea, it was in the context of parenting. Don Dinkmeyer and Gary McKay, building on the work of Alfred Adler, introduced it in their *STEP (Systematic Training for Effective Parenting)* programs. It was designed to help parents avoid doing too much *for* their children — to stop rescuing, over-controlling, or taking on problems that children needed to handle for themselves. But over the years, I've found this idea applies *everywhere*: marriage, work, friendships, ministry, and especially in how we lead and walk with other men. The basic idea is this: Before reacting to a problem, pause and ask yourself — *Who owns this problem?* That single question can completely change how you respond.

Here's why it matters:

> 1. It clarifies responsibility. We stop jumping in just because we *feel* tension. We ask: *Whose life is this problem impacting most directly?* That's the owner.

> 2. It calibrates your role. Not every problem is yours to fix. Some require action, some require empathy, and some just require your silence and support.

> 3. It sets boundaries. And boundaries are not walls — they're bridges. They define where you end and where someone else begins. They protect freedom, dignity, and responsibility.

Let's walk through the three main categories — and how each one calls for a different kind of response.

When the Problem Is Yours

> You own the problem when:

> You are the one directly affected.

> Your boundaries are being violated.

You're feeling the tension, the stress, the consequences of someone else's actions.

Maybe your coworker consistently dumps last-minute tasks on your desk. Maybe your teenage son is leaving the kitchen a disaster every night after you've asked for help. Maybe your wife is routinely making financial decisions without consulting you. In these cases, *you* are feeling the weight. That means *you* own the problem.

How should you respond? With maturity. With clarity. With love and directness. This is where healthy communication comes in. And Scripture gives us great wisdom here:

> *"If your brother or sister sins, go and point out their fault, just between the two of you." — Matthew 18:15*

Use "I" statements — not accusations or passive-aggressive jabs.

"I feel frustrated when I come home and see dishes piled up after I've worked all day."

"I need us to agree on big purchases before we make them. That's part of how I feel respected and in unity."

These aren't threats. They're invitations to maturity. They're statements of responsibility. Own your feelings. Own your limits. Own your contribution to the problem — and take the initiative to resolve it, not with aggression, but with wisdom and clarity.

When the Problem Belongs to Someone Else

You're going to face this one a lot — especially as a husband and a father. It's the kind of situation that *feels* like a crisis in your hands, but it isn't actually yours to fix.

You know it's not your problem when:

> You're not the one experiencing the consequences.
>
> The other person created the situation.
>
> The other person is the one whose life will be directly affected by the outcome.

Think of your teenage daughter who forgot to study for her history exam and is now panicked the night before. That's *her* problem. She owns the anxiety, the grade, the consequences. Or your friend at church who keeps bouncing between jobs, blaming bad luck but refusing to take feedback. You feel for him — but the instability is *his* burden, not yours.

As a man, especially as a Christian man, you'll *want* to jump in. But if you always carry other people's problems, you're actually robbing them of the opportunity to grow.

This is what Paul meant when he wrote:

> *"Each one should carry their own load."* — Galatians 6:5

That's not harsh. That's holy.

So what's your role?

> Empathy: "That sounds tough."

Active Listening: "Tell me more about how you're feeling."

Offer (Don't Push) Advice: "Would it help to talk through some options? Or do you just need to vent?"

When the Problem Is Shared

These are the big ones. The situations where both parties are affected, invested, and impacted.

Think:

Parenting styles and decisions.

Money management and budgeting.

Division of household responsibilities.

Sex and intimacy.

Spiritual leadership and direction.

In these areas, there's no clean owner. You *both* live in the consequences, so you *both* carry responsibility. These shared problems require something more than empathy. They require partnership.

How do you respond? With teamwork, prayer, and humility. This is where mature men step into co-leadership, not control. Where we say, "Let's figure this out together," not, "Here's what you need to do." You take your ego off the table. You invite the Spirit into the room. You remind yourself: you're not trying to win — you're trying to walk in unity.

Paul's challenge to the church becomes a blueprint for how to navigate shared problems in marriage and family:

> "Do nothing out of selfish ambition or vain conceit. Rather, in humility value others above yourselves... not looking to your own interests but each of you to the interests of the others." — Philippians 2:3-4

So you slow down.

> You listen.
>
> You ask your wife what she needs.
>
> You talk with your kids, not at them.
>
> You pray before you plan.

Shared problems become sacred ground when handled with grace.

The Wisdom of My Friend James

My best friend James has a phrase that perfectly encapsulates this principle. He's said it to his wife, his kids, and me more times than I can count:

> ***"I can't solve your problem for you, but if you want, I can listen and offer advice."***

That's gold. That's the kind of mature, godly masculinity our world needs more of. He's saying, "I see you. I care.

But I respect your agency." He's offering help without control. Guidance without pressure. Let me show you what that looks like.

The Car, the Wife, and the Silence

Michael and his wife Erin had been married for 12 years. Good marriage. Solid communication — most days. But one evening, Erin came home from work, upset.

She sat at the table, sighed, and said, "My supervisor completely dismissed my idea in the meeting today. It was humiliating."

Michael — being a good man — responded instinctively.

"Did you push back? You should've said something. Next time, walk in with a stronger proposal. Maybe I can help you write it out."

Erin went quiet. Not angry. Just... distant.

That night, Michael told their small group leader, "I don't get it. I tried to help."

The leader asked, "Did she ask you to solve it?"

"No... she just told me what happened."

"Then she probably wanted you to listen, not fix it."

Lightbulb.

The next evening, Erin brought it up again. This time, Michael leaned in, looked her in the eye, and said, "That sounds awful. Do you want me to listen, or would it help to brainstorm together?"

She smiled. "Just listen."

That simple shift changed the tone of their marriage. Why? Because Michael learned to recognize: he didn't own the problem. Erin did. His role was presence, not control.

The Teen with the Broken Grade

A father named Andre found his 16-year-old son Caleb staring at a math test with a big red "F" at the top.

"I failed," Caleb mumbled.

Andre felt a surge of frustration. "What happened? Didn't we go over the material?"

"I thought I had it... I just froze."

Andre took a breath. He'd been working hard on not rushing in.

"Do you want help figuring out what went wrong, or do you just need to vent?"

Caleb looked surprised. "I don't know. I guess... maybe both."

So they talked. Andre didn't give a lecture. He didn't call the teacher. He sat with his son in the disappointment.

Later, Caleb said, "Thanks for not making it worse. I just needed a minute."

Andre knew something vital: his son owned the problem — and that's how Caleb would grow.

When the Problem Is Your Wife's — And You Can't Fix It

Let me talk to the husbands for a moment — and I include myself in this.

There are few things that make a man feel more helpless than seeing his wife in pain and not being able to make it better. Whether it's stress from her job, tension with her family, anxiety about the kids, or something deeper and more internal — as men, we feel that pressure in our bones.

We want to take the weight off her shoulders. We want to shield her from anything that hurts. That's not pride. That's love. That's a godly instinct.

But sometimes — and this is hard to accept — you can't fix it.

And the truth is: you weren't meant to.

This is one of the great growth points in Christian marriage: learning to be present in your wife's pain without rushing to solve it. It's realizing that emotional leadership often means *sitting with* rather than *acting on*.

I remember a conversation with a man in one of my counseling groups. His wife had recently gone through a miscarriage. She was grieving, silently and deeply. He kept suggesting things: "Let's take a trip. Let's pray together more. Let's go see a counselor."

All good things. But she wasn't ready for any of it.

One night she finally said, "I need you to stop trying to fix this and just sit with me in it."

That broke him. But it also freed him.

Because the truth is, sometimes what your wife needs most is your presence, not your prescription.

She needs to feel that you're *with her* — emotionally, spiritually, and physically — even when you can't take the pain away.

Look at Jesus with Mary and Martha. He didn't jump straight into fixing their grief over Lazarus. He wept with them. (John 11:35)

There will be times your wife carries pain you can't remove. And in those moments, your role is to mirror Christ — not by doing, but by abiding. By holding space. By being safe and steady and present.

Your silent strength in those moments speaks louder than a thousand sermons.

The Weight of the Ministry Wife

Let me share a story from a couple I once walked with — Jared and Melissa.

Jared was a youth pastor. His wife Melissa led worship at their church. From the outside, they looked like the perfect ministry couple: talented, devoted, always smiling.

But privately, Melissa was struggling. The expectations, the criticisms, the gossip behind her back about her song choices, her style, even how she dressed — it all added up. She was exhausted, emotionally raw, and starting to pull away.

One night after church, she came home, dropped her bag by the door, and said, "I don't know how much more of this I can take."

Jared's blood pressure shot up. He felt like he had to *do something*. Should he go to the elders? Defend her from the pulpit? Call a meeting?

But something in him said, Wait.

So instead, he took a breath and asked, "Do you want me to fix this, or do you just want me to hear you right now?"

She looked up with tired eyes and said, "Just hear me."

So he did. He sat with her on the couch. He put his arm around her. He said nothing for a long time. And when she was ready, she told him everything.

That night, she didn't walk away from ministry — she stepped deeper into trust, because her husband knew the difference between fixing and faithfully being with her.

Brothers, sometimes your wife doesn't need a protector or a preacher. She needs a partner. A presence. A man who knows how to sit on the ash heap beside her, like Job's friends *almost* got right — before they started talking.

A Biblical Foundation

You don't have to look far in Scripture to see the model of emotional maturity in Jesus. He wasn't just the Savior of the world — He was the best listener the world had ever known.

When the rich young ruler came to Him with questions, Jesus looked at him and loved him, even though He knew the man would walk away (Mark 10:21).

When the woman at the well poured out her brokenness, Jesus didn't cut her off with a solution — He led her gently to the truth, one layer at a time (John 4).

When Mary and Martha wept over their brother Lazarus, Jesus didn't rebuke their sorrow — He entered it. He cried with them.

Jesus had the power to fix anything instantly. But He didn't always rush to solve — because He understood what people needed most: to be seen, heard, and loved.

That's what we're called to as men of God.

Not to be the savior — Jesus already has that job. Not to be the answer — Scripture already gives us that. But to be men who reflect the character of Christ:

> Steady in presence.
>
> Slow to speak.
>
> Quick to listen.
>
> Strong enough to wait.

James 1:19 says it plainly:

> "Everyone should be quick to listen, slow to speak and slow to become angry."

That's not just a verse for conflict. It's a blueprint for maturity. And it applies everywhere: in marriage, fatherhood, ministry, and brotherhood.

The art of **emotional presence** — of discerning when to speak and when to be silent — is a form of spiritual leadership. It takes wisdom. It takes the Holy Spirit. And yes, it takes humility.

Maturity Is Knowing When to Step In — and When to Sit Down

Let's pull all this together. As men, we like clarity. We like action. We like measurable wins. But life — and especially relationships — doesn't always work like that. You can't chart spiritual growth on a whiteboard. You can't fix grief with a three-point plan. You can't build trust with a well-crafted speech. Sometimes, the strongest thing you can do is listen well, love deeply, and walk humbly. Let me say that again, because it's countercultural: The strongest thing you can do may be to say nothing and simply stay close.

So let's return to our core idea: Before you rush to act, ask yourself: "Who owns this problem?" If it's yours, own it. Lead with integrity and truth. If it's theirs, support them. Listen. Encourage. Offer advice — only if they want it. If it's shared, approach it as a team. Shoulder it together with prayer and mutual respect. And if it's your wife's — and you can't solve it — don't panic. Just *be there*.

You were made to build. To protect. To lead. But you were not made to carry **every** burden — or to rob others of the growth that comes from carrying their own. Wisdom is knowing the difference. It takes humility to say, "That's not mine to fix." It takes strength to say, "I'll sit with you in this, even when I can't solve it." It takes love to listen more than you speak.

Be that kind of man. The kind who knows that maturity isn't measured by how many problems you fix — but by how wisely, prayerfully, and faithfully you choose which ones to carry. Let that be your banner as a man of character. Not controlling. Not distant. Not passive. Not reactive. But faithful. Wise. Grounded. And most of all, present.

Because that's what the people in your life really need — not a perfect man, but *present* man.

Scriptures for Reflection:

- Galatians 6:2,5 — Bearing one another's burdens vs. carrying one's own load.

- Proverbs 20:5 — "The purposes of a person's heart are deep waters, but one who has insight draws them out."

- James 1:19 — "Everyone should be quick to listen, slow to speak and slow to become angry."

- Ecclesiastes 3:7 — "A time to be silent and a time to speak."

I will leave you with the words of my friend James, who puts it so well — "I can't solve your problem for you, but if you want, I can listen and offer advice."

Field Notes:

1. Situation Report:

Where did this chapter hit home for me?

2. Operational Insight:

What truth or principle stands out to me the most?

3. Action Step:

What's one small thing I will do differently this week because of this chapter?

4. Words to Say:

Who needs to hear something from me?

5. Brief Prayer:

Write a one-sentence prayer asking God to strengthen your character in this area.

Endless Exhaustion:
The Toll of Loving an Ungrateful Heart

Have you ever been in a relationship where you gave everything you had—your time, your energy, your patience—only to watch the person you cared for continue to stumble and fall, no matter how much you helped? Have you poured your heart into offering advice and support, only to be met with indifference, resentment, or blame? If you've ever sat in stunned silence, wondering how your love could be so invisible to someone you've given everything to, you're not alone.

This chapter is for every man who has ever tried to love someone who couldn't—or wouldn't—love them back. It's for the fathers whose sacrifices were never acknowledged, the husbands whose care was met with contempt, and the brothers and friends whose loyalty went unnoticed. It's also for the man who is starting to wonder if he's become that person himself—someone whose heart has grown ungrateful and entitled.

Gratitude is not just a warm feeling—it's a cornerstone of character. It shapes the way we receive love, respond to correction, and give back to the people who invest in us. And when it's missing, everything breaks down. This chapter will walk through the anatomy of gratitude and ingratitude, and the way each either fosters life or destroys connection.

The Hidden Cost of Loving Without Return

Let me tell you about Kevin. He came into my counseling office slumped, emotionally drained, and carrying the weight of a failing marriage. He had tried everything: weekend getaways, marriage retreats, personal change, open conversations. His wife, however, remained cold. She criticized more than she appreciated, ignored his efforts, and withheld affection while making demands. Kevin wasn't perfect, but he was sincere. And he was exhausted.

"No matter what I do," he said, "she acts like it's never enough. And I don't think she even sees me anymore."

What Kevin didn't yet have words for was that he was living with the slow decay caused by ingratitude. When a man's sacrificial love is met not with warmth or even acknowledgment, but with a cold void of entitlement, it doesn't just hurt—it hollows him out. Gratitude, when present, refreshes the soul of both giver and receiver. But ingratitude—particularly from someone close—becomes a psychological erosion. And the longer it goes on, the more a man begins to doubt his own value.

This is why recognizing the presence—or absence—of gratitude is so essential. We tend to minimize it, to think of it as a polite behavior rather than a vital sign of relational health. But gratitude—or the lack of it—often tells us more about the future of a relationship than any other trait.

Gratitude: Strength in Humility

At its core, gratitude is strength cloaked in humility. It's the ability to see beyond yourself and recognize the goodness in others. A grateful heart says, "I see what you've done for me. I know you didn't have to. And I receive it with honor."

This isn't about false modesty or being overly sentimental. Gratitude is fiercely practical. It keeps us grounded. It teaches us to be teachable. It makes us less defensive, more connected, and more likely to grow. It helps us see people as allies, not opponents. And it's the fertile soil in which strong character grows.

A grateful man can hear hard truths. He can accept feedback without folding into shame or lashing out in anger. He can receive love without questioning whether he deserves it. That kind of security produces emotional maturity, and emotional maturity is what makes a man reliable—in friendship, in fatherhood, in marriage, in life.

The Ungrateful Heart: When Entitlement Takes Root

The ungrateful heart sees the world through a different lens. Rather than viewing gifts as blessings, it sees them as debts being repaid. Rather than seeing feedback as an opportunity, it sees it as an insult. It lives in a mindset of scarcity: nothing is ever enough, and everyone is either a competitor or a disappointment.

Let me introduce you to Brandon. He was the kind of man who couldn't take a compliment without suspicion and couldn't take criticism without anger. When his boss told him he had room to grow in leadership, Brandon heard disrespect. When his wife surprised him with a birthday dinner, he grumbled that she invited the wrong people. Gratitude was foreign to him—and so was joy.

Brandon's life was a slow burn of resentment. He felt overlooked, underappreciated, and constantly misunderstood. But the truth is, he had slowly trained himself to see only what was missing. His ungratefulness wasn't circumstantial—it was spiritual. It was a condition of the heart that made love impossible to recognize and correction impossible to receive.

And here's the scary part: men like Brandon often don't realize they're ungrateful. In their minds, they're just being honest, just telling it like it is. But in truth, they're robbing themselves of peace, connection, and personal growth.

Feedback or Fight? The Test of Gratitude

One of the most revealing tests of a man's character is how he responds to feedback. A grateful man hears critique and—though it might sting—pauses to ask, "Is there truth in this?" He might not agree with everything, but he stays open. He respects the fact that someone took the time to invest in his growth.

But the ungrateful heart? It bristles. It fights. It often explodes.

There's a term in psychology called "narcissistic rage." It describes the intense anger that some people experience when they feel criticized, even mildly. For them, feedback isn't a gift—it's an attack. And the response is swift: blame, denial, deflection, or stonewalling.

Many men wouldn't classify themselves as narcissists, but we've all seen this kind of rage. Some of us have lived it. When a man can't bear the discomfort of being corrected, he loses his chance to grow. Worse, he often alienates the very people who care enough to speak truth into his life.

A grateful heart, by contrast, welcomes truth. It doesn't always agree immediately—but it listens. It respects the process. And over time, it becomes wiser, stronger, and more resilient. Gratitude isn't about being soft—it's about being steady.

The Relational Fallout of Ingratitude

Every relationship operates on the fragile balance of give and take. Gratitude is what fuels that cycle. When one person gives and the other acknowledges it, the bond strengthens. But when appreciation disappears, the entire system starts to collapse.

In marriage, ingratitude breeds bitterness. In friendship, it creates distance. In parenting, it erodes influence. Over time, the giver begins to pull back—not out of spite, but out of self-preservation. And what's left is a hollow, transactional shell of what the relationship once was.

Gratitude protects against that decay. It says, "I see you. I value what you've done. I don't take it for granted."

In my years as a counselor, I've seen more relationships fall apart due to ingratitude than to betrayal. Not because gratitude was intentionally withheld, but because it was never practiced. And like any muscle, what isn't used eventually atrophies.

Becoming a Grateful Man

So what do we do if we recognize the signs of ingratitude in ourselves? Or what if we've spent years trying to love someone who can't see our heart?

First, we begin with awareness. We take an honest look at our relationships and ask:

- Do I respond with appreciation or expectation?
- Do I welcome correction or resent it?
- Do I acknowledge the love I receive, or do I silently measure what's lacking?

Second, we begin to cultivate gratitude. Not just in words, but in posture. We start saying "thank you" more often—to our wives, our kids, our co-workers, our mentors. We keep a gratitude journal. We push back against the voice of entitlement that says, "I deserve better," and replace it with the heart of humility that says, "I've been given much."

And third, if we're loving someone who refuses to be grateful, we set boundaries. We stop tying our worth to their reactions. We stop offering ourselves as a doormat. We start discerning whether the relationship is built on love—or if it's simply feeding a bottomless pit of entitlement.

Gratitude won't solve every relational challenge, but it will always show you the truth. It will either bring you closer to the people who care about you—or give you the clarity to let go of those who never truly have.

Final Thoughts: The Daily Choice

Every day, we choose between gratitude and entitlement. Between softening our heart or hardening it. Between receiving love with openness—or rejecting it with suspicion.

The grateful heart sees the world clearly. It sees people not as tools or threats, but as gifts. And that clarity leads to wisdom, strength, and the kind of manhood that blesses everyone around him.

So choose gratitude. Not because it's easy—but because it's the only way to build a life worth living. And if you're exhausted from loving someone who refuses to be grateful, take heart. You are not alone—and your love, even when unacknowledged, is never wasted. It has shaped you into someone stronger, more compassionate, and more courageous than you were before.

And that, brother, is something to be deeply grateful for.

Field Notes:

1. Situation Report:

Where did this chapter hit home for me?

2. Operational Insight:

What truth or principle stands out to me the most?

3. Action Step:

What's one small thing I will do differently this week because of this chapter?

4. Words to Say:

Who needs to hear something from me?

5. Brief Prayer:

Write a one-sentence prayer asking God to strengthen your character in this area.

Would You Let Your Son Do That?

It's been a long day. You pull into the driveway, stretch your back a little, and head into the house. The second your hand touches the doorknob, you smell it — beer and cigarette smoke. That's odd. You push open the door and step inside. The living room is hazy. The TV is blaring. You glance toward your recliner, your chair — the one spot you sink into every night — and there he is. Your 15-year-old son. Slouched back, feet kicked up, a cigarette between his fingers, an open beer in his other hand — his fourth, based on the cans next to him. He sees you and smirks.

"Hey, Dad," he says. His speech is loose. His eyes are glassy.

You glance at your wife, standing in the corner. She looks helpless — frustrated, sad, afraid to say more because the last time she did, he snapped at her. Your heart pounds. With anger first — but then with something deeper. Grief. Confusion. How did this happen? What changed in him? What influenced him to think this was okay? And then — the instinct rises. ***No!*** Not in this house. This stops now. Because you know what it leads to — you've seen it in friends and family. Substance dependence, relational damage, a warped view of manhood. You'd sit him down. You'd speak truth, even if it's hard. You'd make changes. Because this — this is serious.

The Family Computer

It's late. You've been tossing and turning, your mind spinning with work stress and family to-do lists. You finally give in, swing your legs off the bed, and head for the kitchen. As you pass the family room, you notice the glow from the computer screen. Someone's up.

You round the corner quietly and stop in your tracks. It's your 14-year-old son. He's seated at the desk, eyes glued to the screen. One hand on the mouse. The other… you don't want to see, but you do. He's watching pornography. You freeze. The room seems to spin for a second. He hasn't seen you yet.

A part of you wants to yell. Another part wants to walk away and pretend you didn't see it. But you don't. You step in. He jumps. Scrambles to close the screen. Stutters. You don't raise your voice. Not yet. You just ask, "How long has this been going on?"

He can't look at you. Your heart breaks. Not just because of what he's done, but because of what it means — about what he's being shaped by, about what he's learning to associate with manhood and sexuality.

You wouldn't let it slide. You'd get help. You'd walk with him. Because you know this kind of habit won't just stay on the screen. It will reach into his future relationships, his understanding of love, his ability to connect. And you love him too much to let that happen.

The Credit Card Bill

You're sitting at the kitchen table, coffee in hand, flipping through the bills. You open the credit card statement and blink twice. $3,672. You stare harder. You read the line items. Online gambling. Sports betting apps. Casino platforms. Your stomach drops. It's the emergency card. The one you gave to your 16-year-old son, just in case. He's never used it recklessly before. But this — this is more than a mistake. This is a pattern.

You walk into his room and hold out the bill. "What's this?"

He stammers. Tries to explain. He didn't think it would get that bad. He thought he could win it back. He didn't think you'd notice. And now your budget is wrecked. Your wife is furious. The money that was set aside for groceries, gas, and the overdue car repair? Gone.

You sit down at the edge of his bed. You're not just mad. You're disappointed. You trusted him. He had access, and he abused it. But more than anything, you're afraid for what this means. For the kind of man he's becoming if he doesn't learn self-control. If he doesn't learn discipline and responsibility. So you take action. You restrict access. You require accountability. You lay out consequences. Because that's what good fathers do.

The Hallway

It's deep in the night when you hear the sound. A thud. Then a distant voice. Then something that makes the hair on your arms stand up. You grab the bat from under your bed and quietly make your way upstairs. You move down the hall, toward the sound. You reach your 17-year-old son's door. You knock once. No answer. You push it open. And what you see drops your heart to the floor. Your son is in bed with a woman you've never seen before. Clothes scattered. No shame. No explanation. He scrambles. She covers herself. You stand there, stunned.

You walk out, not even sure what to say.

Later, you have the conversation. You ask him how he thought this was okay. You talk about honor, about purity, about what kind of man treats sex like a game. You talk about the damage — to her, to him, to your trust. And you tell him: this isn't about rules. It's about who he's becoming. Because you know the truth: sexual sin doesn't just mess with behavior. It twists identity. And it doesn't just show up — it grows in the dark, where no one is paying attention. So you tell him the truth. And you walk him toward repentance. Because that's what a father does.

Now, let me ask you a question — not to guilt you, not to shame you, but to wake something up inside you. Would you let your son do al those things that you allow yourself to do? Think about that for a second. Really sit with it. Would you let your son treat his future wife the way you treat yours in your worst moments? Would you be okay watching him blow off responsibilities, slack on spiritual discipline, blow up in anger, or numb himself with porn, food, or alcohol? Would you smile and say, "Boys will be boys," or would something rise up in you and say, "Son, this isn't who you are. You're better than this."

You probably know where I'm going. That same passion you'd bring to correct him? That urgency? That strength? It's time to point it at yourself. Because the hard truth is, many of us hold our sons — real or imagined — to a higher standard than we hold ourselves. And when that happens, something starts to rot in the roots of who we are. Hypocrisy grows quietly, even in good men, when we forget that the standard we hold for others should first be applied to the man in the mirror. So let's walk through this together. Not to shame you — I'm not interested in that. But to help you wake up, take stock, and walk in the kind of self-control that God uses to shape real men of strength and substance.

Look in the Mirror

Okay, brother. Let's shift the camera. Now imagine the man in these stories is **you**.

- Four beers deep on a weeknight, brushing off your wife's concern with sarcasm.

- Alone with your phone or laptop at 1:00 a.m., scrolling porn and thinking, "It's not hurting anyone."

- Racking up credit card debt on selfish purchases, blaming stress, while your wife sacrifices to keep the family afloat.

- Living in passive rebellion, watching trash on TV, indulging your lust or anger or laziness, and then snapping at your kids for the same behavior.

- These stories hit close to home. Stories that force the question: *"Would I let my son do that?"* I know, you are saying, "he's a kid, its not age appropriate." But ask yourself, why not? What does age have to do with smoking, or sex, or beer, or gambling? Isn't it really that we know that these things are bad for him, and will destroy him if they latch on to him as habits in his life. Don't we truly know that disrespecting his mother and women is a sickness that will destroy his marriage, his example as a father, and his treatment of people in general? Aren't we aware that his self-indulgence places him in opposition to the plan God has for him? If all of this is true for your son, is it also not true for you? What does age have to do with it? Nothing really, except that we have constructed a magic line at eighteen where we take the responsibility on ourselves before, and then leave it on him after. But the cause and effect are the same, regardless of age. Eighteen or eighty, the sickness is the same.

Would you let your son live like that? Would you make excuses for him? Would you say, "That's just what guys do"? No. You'd call him out to a higher level of responsibility and social awareness. So why, then, do you settle for it in yourself?

Your Soul Was Made for More

This isn't about condemnation. This is about *clarity*. This is about loving yourself enough to stop playing games. You are a man. A husband. A father. A son of the living God. You've been called to lead, to love, to protect — not just others, but yourself. The double standard stops today. Let the same fire that would defend your son's future be the fire that refines your own. Let the same conviction that would correct your child correct your heart.

Father Yourself the Way God Fathers You

When Jesus called His followers to self-control, it wasn't about image — it was about love. He knows what sin does. He knows it drains your soul, wrecks your relationships, dims your witness, and eats away at your calling. So He invites you into something better: **discipline, wisdom, and wholeness.**

> "For the Spirit God gave us does not make us timid, but gives us power, love and self-discipline." — 2 Timothy 1:7

He's not calling you to be perfect overnight. He's calling you to walk as a son. A beloved son. A son worth fighting for.

Ask yourself hard questions. Would I let my son watch what I watch? Talk how I talk? Pray as little as I pray?

Name the areas where you've made excuses. Don't dress it up. Call it what it is.

Ask God to father you. Let Him discipline you in love. Let Him call you out — and call you home.

Surround yourself with men who sharpen you. No more hiding. No more pretending. Find brothers who will hold you to the standard you know is right.

Treat yourself like a son you love. Stop coddling your sin. Start coaching your soul.

Brother, you wouldn't let your son keep living that way. Don't let yourself. Your family needs a whole man. Your church needs a godly man. Your God already sees a redeemed man — if you'll let Him shape you. So next time you're tempted to indulge, ask yourself: ***Would I let my son do this?*** If the answer is no — then love yourself enough to say no, too.

Field Notes:

1. Situation Report:
Where did this chapter hit home for me?

2. Operational Insight:
What truth or principle stands out to me the most?

3. Action Step:
What's one small thing I will do differently this week because of this chapter?

4. Words to Say:
Who needs to hear something from me?

5. Brief Prayer:
Write a one-sentence prayer asking God to strengthen your character in this area.

Are You A David, or an Albert?

David and Albert were brothers, raised in the lap of privilege. Their father, a formidable man of influence, had long determined their destinies. David, the elder, was his pride—groomed from birth to inherit the family's legacy. Every advantage was lavished upon him, every indulgence permitted. He was taught not only how to lead but how to be admired, his charm and confidence cultivated like a rare gem.

Albert, by contrast, was an afterthought. Shy, unassuming, and plagued by a quiet nervousness, he was tolerated rather than treasured. Their father viewed his timidity with thinly veiled disappointment, dismissing him as weak and inconsequential. While David was nurtured for greatness, Albert was left to his own devices, expected merely to exist in the shadow of his brother's inevitability.

As the years passed, their differences became stark. David embraced the privileges of his position with reckless abandon—parties, women, and all manner of excess. He was the golden son who could do no wrong, and he knew it. Responsibility was something for the future. For now, he would revel in pleasure.

Albert, however, took another path. He found solace in steadiness, in love, in family. He married a good woman and built a life of quiet contentment, far removed from his brother's world of fleeting indulgence. While David's name filled the headlines with scandal, Albert was unknown, save for those who mattered most to him.

Then, one day, everything changed. Their father died.

David, at last, stood as the head of the family enterprise. The wealth, the power, the authority—it was all his. No longer was there a guiding hand to temper his inclinations. He was free to rule as he pleased. And so, he did.

He surrounded himself with enablers, none more influential than a woman who shared his appetite for indulgence. She was captivating, intoxicating, and, above all, powerful in her own way. She did not merely stand at his side—she took the reins. Unwilling to be confined by convention, she wielded influence that was neither earned nor granted but simply taken. She whispered in David's ear, steered his decisions, and emboldened his worst impulses.

At first, the firm weathered his excesses. But soon, his neglect grew impossible to ignore. The enterprise was more than just his plaything; it was a legacy, one that countless others depended upon. The senior advisors watched in growing alarm as David prioritized pleasure over duty, passion over responsibility. His recklessness was not merely a private matter—it threatened the very stability of the institution.

A confrontation was inevitable. The directors called him to account. He had a choice to make: rise to the station for which he had been prepared all his life, or continue down the path of indulgence, prioritizing his personal desires over the greater good.

The weight of the moment pressed upon him. He could see the disappointment in their eyes, the unspoken truth hanging in the air. They did not believe he would choose duty. And they were right.

Faced with the burden of responsibility, David faltered. He could not bear the thought of losing her, of forsaking his own pleasure for the cold mantle of leadership. He surrendered—not to duty, but to desire. He walked away.

And so, the unthinkable happened. The torch passed to the overlooked son, the quiet one, the boy his father had dismissed as weak. Albert, the reluctant leader, was now thrust into a role he had never sought.

But where David had chased fleeting passions, Albert embraced something greater: duty. And in doing so, he changed the course of history.

For this was no ordinary family. This was no mere enterprise.

David was not simply a wayward heir—he was Edward VIII, King of England. And Albert, the forgotten younger brother, became King George VI.

And so, it was not the charming prince who led his people through their darkest hour, but the hesitant, humble man who never imagined he would wear the crown.

History would remember the choice David made. But it would honor the one Albert embraced.

For where one man abdicated leadership to indulge a woman, another bore the weight leadership to the benefit of a nation.

And now, dear brother, let me ask you to linger for a moment longer in this story.

You've just walked through a tale of two brothers—David and Albert—whose lives diverged not by circumstance alone, but by character. In the corridors of power and privilege, one chose indulgence. The other, duty. One leaned into himself, into the pull of desire and ego. The other stood, shaking perhaps, but faithful. If you have not seen it, watch the movie, The King's Speech. Albert's story is there for all to see where he found himself, and the crisis of his life.

But for now, I wonder—where do *you* find *yourself* in *this* moment? I don't mean in a palace. I mean in your kitchen, your office, your quiet thoughts. I mean in the relationships you steward, in the responsibilities you've been given, in the corners of your character that only you and the Lord can see.

There is a David in all of us—that voice that tempts us to live for our own appetites. The one who whispers, *"You deserve this. Let them wait."* It's the inner monarch who resists accountability and seeks escape. Maybe your David shows up in smaller ways: the scroll on your phone that keeps you from engaging with your kids, the sarcasm that shields you from true vulnerability, the plans you keep pushing off to tomorrow because today you'd rather coast.

But I believe there is also an Albert inside you—perhaps quieter, less self-assured, but grounded. The one who loves deeply, who wants to do what is right even when it is unseen, even when it is hard. The one who might not *feel* ready, but shows up anyway.

I think of a man I once counseled—we'll call him James. James wasn't a king, but he was a husband, a father, and the operations manager at a small construction firm. By his own admission, he had spent the better part of his 30s playing at life. Ambition and charm came easily. But he kept waiting for a "bigger stage" before stepping fully into the man he wanted to be. And when his father passed—suddenly, unexpectedly—it was as if the baton had been dropped into his hands. Not just the family business, but the family itself. His mother's grief. His younger siblings' uncertainty. A church community that looked to him for calm.

He told me once, tears in his eyes, "I didn't want this kind of leadership. I wanted the kind that comes with applause."

But he showed up anyway. He stepped into the quiet, the grind, the emotional labor. And slowly, he discovered something deeper than applause—he discovered legacy.

Brother, this is not just about kings. It's about what kind of man you are becoming when no one is watching. What voices you heed when your comfort competes with your calling. What kind of inheritance you'll leave—not in bank accounts or business portfolios—but in the character you cultivate daily.

Jesus, our true King, wore no silk robe in His moment of glory. He knelt with a towel and washed feet. He bore the weight of a crown not made of gold, but of thorns. And He did not abdicate His mission—not even when it cost Him everything.

So let me gently ask: Where are you choosing desire over duty? Where are you hesitating to rise—not because you're unqualified—but because you've convinced yourself you're not the one? What legacy would your family, your friends, your God remember if today was the day you were called to step forward? If Albert could lead a nation through war, not because he was bold, but because he was faithful—might you lead your family, your church, your life, with that same quiet courage? Because history will remember the crowns we put down. But heaven will honor the crosses we carry.

Field Notes:

1. Situation Report:
Where did this chapter hit home for me?

2. Operational Insight:
What truth or principle stands out to me the most?

3. Action Step:
What's one small thing I will do differently this week because of this chapter?

4. Words to Say:
Who needs to hear something from me?

5. Brief Prayer:
Write a one-sentence prayer asking God to strengthen your character in this area.

You Don't Say

Most men I've counseled over the years are not cruel men. They're not malicious, calculating, or bent on emotional harm. They're working, showing up, trying to hold it together in a world that often gives them no points for effort. So, when they sit across from me—shoulders slumped, voice low, often stunned by what their wives or children have said about how unloved or unseen they feel—I hear a common refrain:

> "But I never said anything bad."

> "I didn't *do* anything wrong."

"I never meant to hurt anyone."

And I believe them. But here's the thing about silence—it's not neutral. It speaks, whether we intend it to or not.

My father used to tell *dad jokes*, maybe yours did too. One of his favorites goes like this...

> A wife was complaining to her husband, "You never tell me you love me."
>
> The husband, indignantly replied, "Wife, I told you I loved you the day we were married. If anything changes, I'll let you know."

This joke in particular was very funny to him. I suppose back in the 50s and 60s it was. It always got a chuckle at the family cookouts. But I'll tell you something—I've seen the wreckage that kind of thinking can leave behind. What makes this sad is the truth behind the joke. Many men do not understand or value the importance of the spoken word when it comes to women and children. Beyond the spoken word, there is action, which men do tend to value, but words are still vital.

Now, in his generation, that joke might've made more sense. Words weren't as cheap then, and people often did more than they said. Still, the truth behind the humor—that love doesn't need to be spoken often—has not aged well. Not in a time when words are the lifeblood of connection. Not in a culture where affirmation is a rare commodity and everyone's starved for it, especially inside the walls of our own homes.

I remember a man named Craig. Stoic, hardworking, never missed a paycheck. He had three kids and a wife who stayed home and did everything she could to keep the family running. Craig didn't yell. He wasn't violent or unfaithful. In his mind, he was doing everything a good husband should do. But when his wife filed for separation, it knocked him flat. "I don't understand," he said. "I've always been faithful. I've never said anything mean. I don't drink or hit or run around. What else does she want from me?"

The answer? She wanted to be loved out loud.

It's not that Craig never *loved* her. It's that she didn't *hear* it. Didn't feel it. Not in the language she needed. And so, to her, it was as if the love wasn't there at all.

Words matter, my friend. And not just the big ones—"I love you" and "I'm proud of you" and "I'm sorry." But the small ones too. "Tell me about your day." "You matter to me." "I'm here." Words are like water to the soul. Without them, even the strongest trees begin to wither.

When I was training therapeutic foster parents, I would tell them something that always raised eyebrows: "These kids need ten hugs a day." Now, a lot of those kids had trauma—real trauma—and a physical hug wasn't always welcome or appropriate. But that wasn't the point. A hug, in that context, was any act of nurture. A moment of connection. A touch, a kind word, a glance that said "you're safe here." You'd be amazed what one small moment of genuine presence can do to a wounded heart.

The same is true in your home. Your children may not need a lecture—but they do need to know they are seen. Your wife may not need you to fix all her problems—but she longs to be reassured she's still loved. And not just with actions, but with words. Not once, years ago, in your wedding vows. But now. Often. Clearly.

There's a moment in Scripture that always catches me. It's when the Father speaks over Jesus at His baptism. Jesus hadn't preached a sermon yet. Hadn't healed a leper or walked on water. But what did the Father say?

"This is my beloved Son, in whom I am well pleased."

If the Son of God needed to *hear* His Father's love, how much more do our sons and daughters? Our wives? Our brothers in Christ?

I'll leave you with this.

One night, I was praying with a man—let's call him Richard—who had grown up in a house with no affection, no affirmation. He had carried that silence like a wound for decades, never realizing how much it shaped the way he fathered his own children. That night, he wept—not for what was said, but for what never was. "I just wish I had known that silence could hurt too."

So let me gently ask you, man to man, counselor to friend:

Is your silence saying more than you realize?

Are there words that need to be spoken—to your wife, to your children, to your Father in Heaven?

Because saying nothing is never saying nothing. And sometimes, the quietest lips speak the loudest wounds.

You don't have to be a poet. You just have to show up with your words. Give voice to the love you already carry. Wrap your family in verbal hugs, whether they know how to ask for them or not.

Because what goes unsaid today might echo for a lifetime.

And so we return to that sacred truth: what goes unsaid today might echo for a lifetime.

The man you are becoming is shaped not only by your work ethic or how you stand under pressure—but by how you speak, and whether you speak at all. You may feel more comfortable with action than with language. Many men do. We're taught to "show, don't tell." Fix it. Build it. Provide. And those things matter deeply. But I'll tell you this, friend—what you *say* is often the bridge that allows those actions to be received with love, rather than obligation.

Take Daniel, for instance. A military man, raised in a house where emotion was considered weakness and words were used only for commands. He was solid. Reliable. But when he came to see me, it wasn't because his hands were failing—it was because his words never showed up. His teenage daughter had pulled away. His wife had grown weary. They felt like boarders in a house where love was presumed but never spoken.

When we talked, Daniel said something I'll never forget:

"I thought I was giving them a fortress. Turns out, I gave them a silence they had to live in."

And that's the thing, isn't it? We assume they know. We assume our presence, our effort, our coming home every night is evidence enough. And sometimes, it *is*. But even stone walls crumble without maintenance. Even the strongest towers feel empty without sound inside.

Words keep the connection alive.

Scripture tells us, "Death and life are in the power of the tongue" (Proverbs 18:21). That's not metaphor. That's truth. A kind word can disarm a child's shame. A moment of verbal blessing can heal a wound that's decades old. A simple, "I'm proud of you," from a father's lips can echo in a boy's heart long after that father has gone to glory.

The tongue may be small, but it steers the ship.

Now, I know some of you reading this are thinking, *"It's just not me. I wasn't raised like that. I'm not good with words."* And that may be true. But brother, neither was Moses. He told God, "I'm slow of speech." And God still chose him to speak for a nation.

Your Father in Heaven is not asking you to be eloquent. He's asking you to be faithful. To speak life where silence has taken root. To open your mouth when it would be easier to walk away. To choose connection, even when it feels foreign to you.

I remember praying with a man in his sixties—his name was Thomas. His marriage had gone cold. Not from betrayal, but from years of distance. No major storms—just fog. You know the kind. Conversations reduced to logistics. "Did you pay the bill?" "What time is dinner?" That sort of thing.

He told me, "I just don't know how to talk anymore. It's been too long."

But the Lord has a way of bringing resurrection where we've long buried things. I told Thomas to start small. I asked him to begin praying *out loud* for his wife—not in some long, formal way, but a few quiet sentences at night. And he did. That first prayer was clumsy. He stumbled. Fumbled. But he spoke. And her tears did the rest.

Because it's not about perfection. It's about presence.

Can I ask you, friend, what words need to be said in your home today?

Is there a son who's been waiting to hear that he's not just tolerated, but *admired*?

Is there a daughter who's been aching to know that she's not a burden, but a delight?

Is there a wife, worn thin by daily battles, who needs to hear, not just that you're still here—but that you still *see* her?

You don't need a degree in counseling to speak life. You just need a heart turned toward Christ—and the courage to let that heart speak.

I often say to men in my office: *Don't wait for a crisis to become communicative. Don't wait for the marriage to be on the rocks, or for your children to be strangers, before you realize how much your words matter.*

The time to speak is *now*. Even if your voice shakes. Even if your pride resists. Even if your own father never spoke a word of love to you.

Because this is your turn. Your field. Your watch.

You can begin again—today—with one sentence. One effort. One holy risk.

And if you're still unsure of where to start, may I offer the simplest of beginnings?

Tell them what your Father told His Son:

"You are my beloved. In you, I am well pleased."

Say it. Mean it. Let it be a healing flood.

Guided Reflection: Speaking Life

Take a moment, brother. Put the book down after this page if you need to. Get somewhere quiet. If you're holding your coffee or sitting in the truck before work, let this next section be just between you and the Lord. Breathe. Slow down.

You don't need a notebook—though you're welcome to grab one. What you do need is honesty.

Let's start here:

Picture the people God has entrusted to your care.

Not the ones you're trying to impress, but the ones who will remember your voice long after you're gone. Your wife, if you're married. Your children. Maybe a friend or a fatherless young man you're mentoring. Who are they? One by one, hold their faces in your mind.

Ask the Lord to bring to mind *one* person who may not know the depth of your love—because you haven't said it in a while.

Now consider this:

What have you assumed they already know?

That you're proud of them? That you forgive them? That you still delight in them?

Have you ever told them? Recently? Out loud?

Now turn your heart toward your own story. Think of your own father—whether he was present or not.

What words did *you* long to hear that never came?

"I see you."

"I'm proud of the man you're becoming."

"You are loved—no matter what."

How did that silence shape you? Are you carrying it still?

Now, here's the final part of this reflection:

Ask your Father in Heaven to speak over you.

Open your Bible to Matthew 3:17. Read it slowly. Then sit in silence for a moment, and let the Spirit whisper it to your soul.

"You are my beloved son. In you, I am well pleased."

Let Him say it again, until it settles.

And when it does…

Ask Him to give you the courage to say it to someone else.

Not tomorrow. Not "when the time is right." Today. Even if it's just a sentence. Even if it's awkward. Even if you stumble over the words.

Because what they remember won't be your eloquence.

They'll remember your voice.

Field Notes:

1. Situation Report:
Where did this chapter hit home for me?

2. Operational Insight:
What truth or principle stands out to me the most?

3. Action Step:
What's one small thing I will do differently this week because of this chapter?

4. Words to Say:
Who needs to hear something from me?

5. Brief Prayer:
Write a one-sentence prayer asking God to strengthen your character in this area.

Change Happens In An Instant

Change happens in instant. It happens when you make a *decision* that change must occur. It can take a very-long-time for you to make a decision to make *true change* but the actual change comes in the instant when you make the decision—the true change decision that is.

However, your change, while instantaneous, will not necessarily be accepted by those around you instantaneously. It could take a very long time for them to decide that they're going to accept your change as real, and in doing so change their attitude toward you.

Therefore, you need to understand and rest on the fact that your change is real because you're acting on the change and you're producing different outcomes and you're recognizing your efforts. The change is proven to be real and instantaneous when you change what you're doing as your reaction to your decision to change. It is not dependent upon how other people react to you to prove that your change is real or not real.

People change reluctantly because they fear that the change will not produce what they hope for. Or they fear they will lose too much. Or they fear that they will fail. They fear… And so it takes a long time to make a decision to make a change. Yet, once the decision is actually made the change is instantaneous. Your follow-through will give you proof that you actually made the change.

What others are observing you they may actually notice the change. They may notice the evidence actually, of the change. But, they don't have the inside perspective that you have on why you change, or what you're willing to do to maintain the change, or your heart. They only have the evidence of the change. And the evidence isn't trustworthy unless it's consistent, appropriate, and timely. This means that your evidence has to be a regular occurrence not just a one-time or occasional occurrence. It means it has to be appropriate, or in other words the evidence is actually pointing to the change directly and effectively. And it has to be timely, meaning that it doesn't wait until it's convenient, but it happens in the here and now, and it continues over time until by preponderance of evidence of time, appropriateness, and consistency others will see the change is real and permanent.

Change happens in an instant. The decision to change is where we usually get

stuck.

Field Notes:

1. Situation Report:
Where did this chapter hit home for me?

2. Operational Insight:
What truth or principle stands out to me the most?

3. Action Step:
What's one small thing I will do differently this week because of this chapter?

4. Words to Say:
Who needs to hear something from me?

5. Brief Prayer:
Write a one-sentence prayer asking God to strengthen your character in this area.

Great Marriages Don't Just Happen
Do You Want More than Typical

I have listened to couples talk about their marriage goals for so long now that I couldn't begin to count the numbers the hours or the events. But some things are thematic and constant. When I ask couples to describe their ideal marriage they usually Tell me about their grandparents marriage, or somebody they know from church that had a great marriage where everything seemed to be perfect. They talk about affection, humor, support, and the absence of conflict. They talk about longevity, and mutual goals, and many other things that they can identify for the outside that seem to exemplify their vision of a great marriage. Then I ask them about their own marriage and they usually grow sad and quiet. Most couples don't have anything close to the imagined perfect marriage that they would have. Their love stories are incongruent with their life.

In these cases, my job becomes clear. I need to help this couple recognize the marriage they want to have, recognize the marriage they do have, and then create a process to get from one point to the other. Many of them have a good marriage. A marriage that by all metrics is typical in our culture. Perhaps it's not perfect, perhaps it's not terribly dysfunctional, it's good. But good is not enough for marriage. We want great marriages. After all, the quality of your marriage determines the quality of your life, the quality of your family, the quality of your children's future, and at the end of the race, as you look back, whether or not you had a good marriage or a great marriage determines so much in terms of your life satisfaction.

Great marriages don't just happen however. Great marriages require effort. When I was a child my mother would say to me marriage is a lot of work. When I was a teenager my youth counselors at church said marriage is a lot of work. When I was preparing to get married or premarital counselor said marriage is a lot of work. When marriage got difficult and I would talk to people about my struggles they would remind me that marriage is a lot of work. Okay, I get that. But nobody told me what the work was. And that I think is the most frustrating part. People will tell you marriage is a lot of work, and they probably a referencing their own work. But marriage is a lot of work does not tell us anything. It doesn't give us a method on how to make marriage happen. This book is about making your marriage work by doing the work of the marriage, specifically to go from a good marriage to a great marriage.

Reference good to great by Jim Collins and hit this methodology.

Reference Andy Andrews and just Jones for his methodology.

Field Notes:

1. Situation Report:
Where did this chapter hit home for me?

2. Operational Insight:
What truth or principle stands out to me the most?

3. Action Step:
What's one small thing I will do differently this week because of this chapter?

4. Words to Say:
Who needs to hear something from me?

5. Brief Prayer:
Write a one-sentence prayer asking God to strengthen your character in this area.

Raising the Banner Daily

Brother, if you've made it this far, then you've done more than read—you've wrestled. You've stared at the mirror, considered your habits, and perhaps even heard God's whisper in some uncomfortable places. That's good. That's growth. Because this book was never about tips and techniques—it was about transformation. It was about becoming a man who carries the weight of his name with honor and lives like Christ is not just his Savior, but his King.

The essays you've read are not rules—they're road signs. Not commands—they're counsel. They are field-tested truths from one man to another, forged in the fire of real conversations, real marriages, real regrets, and real victories. You don't need to master every chapter this week. But you do need to pick up the banner. The banner of consistency. Of courage. Of confession. The banner that says, "My life will speak what my mouth professes. My actions will echo my faith. My love will look like Christ."

Every day you wake up, you're flying a flag. Whether in your marriage, your fatherhood, your friendships, or your failures, you are broadcasting what kingdom you serve. Let that flag be unmistakable. Let your wife see it in how you pursue her. Let your children feel it in how you discipline and delight in them. Let your coworkers notice the integrity that doesn't waver when no one's looking. Let your own heart be convicted and comforted by a life that is aligned.

And when you fall short—and you will—return to these pages, not to feel shame, but to find your footing. Start with the *Field Notes*. Reflect. Repent. Reengage. Because masculinity is not proven by perfection. It's proven by presence. And it is measured not by your position, but by the character with which you carry your responsibilities.

So take these words, not as a conclusion, but as a commissioning. Use them like a field manual. A weekly guide. A reminder that you are not alone, that you are not without direction, and that you are not without grace. God has called you to something greater than survival—He has called you to stewardship. Of your home. Your influence. Your heart. And that, my brother, is the edge you were born to sharpen.

Field Notes:

1. Situation Report:
Where did this chapter hit home for me?

2. Operational Insight:
What truth or principle stands out to me the most?

3. Action Step:
What's one small thing I will do differently this week because of this chapter?

4. Words to Say:
Who needs to hear something from me?

5. Brief Prayer:
Write a one-sentence prayer asking God to strengthen your character in this area.

Carry the Flame

You've walked through battlefields of the heart, stood in front of the mirror of truth, and faced the call of character. You've wrestled with identity, misbehavior, legacy, leadership, silence, presence, and pain. But the question remains—what now?

This book was never meant to be a badge of achievement. It was meant to be a blade—sharpening you. And now, it's time to carry it into the world.

A godly man doesn't wait to feel heroic before acting with courage. He moves in obedience, even when he feels unsure. He leads his home, even when he doesn't feel worthy. He chooses integrity, even when no one is watching.

The world is watching. Your wife is watching. Your children are watching. But more than that—God is watching. Not with a clipboard, but with the eyes of a Father who entrusted you with sacred ground.

You are the man God chose for your family. You are the one who carries the torch into a culture that has lost its flame. You are not perfect—but you are chosen.

So take what you've learned here. Live it out loud. Ask forgiveness when you fail. Rise again when you fall. Love deeply. Lead humbly. Fight honorably. And let your life declare: "Christ lives here."

Because in the end, it's not about impressing others with your strength. It's about leaving a trail of blessing that outlives you.

Carry the flame. Light the way.

Thematic Reference Index

1. Authentic Manhood Rooted in Biblical Identity

- *The Conversation of Your Life*
- *Carrying the Banner*
- *Attend to the Tree Not the Fruit*
- *Are You A David, or an Albert?*

2. Spiritual Leadership and Headship in the Home

- *Putting the Horse Before the Cart*
- *Maybe it's time to Pop the Hood on Your Marriage*
- *Great Marriages Don't Just Happen*
- *Would You Let Your Son Do That?*

3. Emotional Presence and Relational Integrity

- *You Don't Say*
- *When She Stopped Smiling* (within *Carrying the Banner*)
- *The Man in the Mirror* (within *Carrying the Banner*)
- *Endless Exhaustion*

4. Maturity Through Repentance, Self-Awareness & Discipleship

- *What Lies Beneath: The Goals of Misbehavior*
- *Trigger Points*
- *Change Happens In An Instant*
- *Feeding The Hungry Man*

5. Living a Consistent, Gospel-Aligned Life

- *The Truth Shall Set You Free*

- *Fruit From a Poisoned Tree*
- *Tomorrow For Sure!*
- *Thinking Outside What Box?*
- *Less is More & When to Not To…*

About the Author

Dr. Chuck Carrington, PhD, EdS, MA, is a Christian therapist, educator, author, and speaker with over 30 years of experience working with couples, families, and individuals—including trauma survivors, foster families and children, men recovering from pornography addiction, and the wives healing from betrayal trauma. He specializes in trauma, grief, and loss, with a focused practice in Christian counseling that emphasizes relational restoration in the wake of betrayal, infidelity, and emotional dysfunction.

Dr. Chuck's research explores innovative approaches to loss recovery, process addictions, betrayal trauma, post-traumatic embitterment, and the long-term impact of childhood family dysfunction. Blending biblical wisdom with evidence-based therapeutic models and a down-to-earth relational style, he brings compassion, clarity, and deep insight into how past wounds shape present relationships.

He is the founder of *Connect Christian Family Counseling*, where he walks alongside clients on their journey toward emotional and relational wholeness.

When he's not writing or counseling, Dr. Chuck enjoys reading, researching, leading workshops, and serving in local ministry projects. He also hosts free online support and discipleship groups. This book reflects his passion for bringing a practical, gospel-centered message to those navigating the complex challenges of modern life—helping them rediscover their identity and purpose in God's redemptive plan, and equipping them to grow in truth, strength, and grace.

If You Need Counseling or Help,

Dr Chuck offers Christian Faith-Based Counseling and Coaching in men's recovery from porn and cyber-addiction, Betrayal Trauma recovery for women, and restorative counseling to help heal and recover marriages after betrayal.

For a consultation via telehealth video, contact Dr Chuck to get more information on how to overcome the damage of betrayal and addiction. Use the website below to sign up for recovery and support groups, or to join Dr Chuck's online psychoeducational programs.

If you are looking for marriage enhancement counseling or coaching, Dr Chuck offers online webinars and forums to help Christian couples explore their marriage, and how it conforms to God's plan for marriage, to find forgiveness and healing, or to plan for an extraordinary marriage from the outset for engaged couples.

Believers should ask for the Faith-based community discount for the best possible pricing. Free groups include Healing Hearts for women damaged by betrayal, Overcomer's Group for men struggling with porn

addiction and cyber addiction.

www.connectcounselor.com
Connect Christian Family Counseling

757 965-5450

Other Titles by Dr Chuck

Feelings Don't Care About Your Facts: How emotional Reasoning Hijacks Logic
ISBN# 979-8-9892386-7-5
Is available on Amazon at

The Renewed Mind: Rebuilding Trust in Marriage by Overcoming Porn Addiction for Life
ISBN# 979-89892386-3-7
Is available on Amazon at
https://a.co/d/7qwOY7h

The Renewed Mind companion workbook
ISBN# 979-8-9892386-2-0 is available on Amazon at
https://a.co/d/fTPdxoO

The Loving Marriage: Jesus Reduce Me To Love. Lessons on living out 1 Corinthians in Marriage is available on Amazon https://a.co/d/eZttPf8
ISBN# 979-8989238651

Check out Dr Chuck's ***Seven Greatest Hits in Marriage Counseling***, a series of video supported coaching modules presenting his most effective tools to help couples exceed a typical marriage.

www.connectcounselor.com
Connect Christian Family Counseling
757 965-5450
DrChuck@connectcounselor.com

www.ingramcontent.com/pod-product-compliance
Lightning Source LLC
Chambersburg PA
CBHW070643160426
43194CB00009B/1565